Active Income Streams:

Side-Income Opportunities for Achieving
Financial Freedom
(Working as Much or as Little as You Desire)

By Kristi Patrice Carter, JD

Active Income Streams: Side-Income Opportunities for Achieving Financial Freedom
(Working as Much or as Little as You Desire)

© **2016 Kristi Patrice Carter, JD**

All rights reserved. No part of this book may be reproduced or transmitted in any form or by any means, electronic or mechanical, including photocopying, recording, or by any information storage and retrieval system, without written permission of the publisher, except in the case of brief quotations embodied in articles or reviews.

Disclaimer

NOTE FROM THE AUTHOR

This book is designed to provide factual information in regard to the subject matter covered. However, it is based on personal experience, interviews with other active-income seekers, and research conducted by the author and her freelance staff. Although much effort was made to ensure that all information in the book is factual and accurate, this book is sold with the understanding that the author assumes no responsibility for oversights, discrepancies, or inaccuracies. This book is not intended to replace financial, investment, legal, accounting, or other professional services. If these services are required, a competent professional should be sought. Readers are reminded to use their own good judgment before applying any ideas presented in this book.

For information, contact:

Thang Publishing Company
332 South Michigan Avenue, Suite 1032, #T610
Chicago, IL 60604-4434

Table of Contents

Acknowledgments 1
Introduction 3
1. Your Success Mind-Set 7
2. Usability Testing 12
3. Writing Content for Cash 21
4. Make Money Writing Reviews and Blogging (Sponsored Posts) .. 28
5. Make Money with Forum-Posting Companies 32
6. Freelancing for Cash 35
7. Nonbidding Freelance Sites 44
8. How To Make Money with Online Chat Jobs 54
9. Make Money with Micro Job Sites 59
10. Make Money as a Customer Support Specialist 69
11. How to Make Money Podcasting 75
12. Making Money Answering Questions Online 79
13. Make Money with Social Media Marketing 82
14. Make Money with Transcription 86
15. Make Money from Home as a Translator 93
16. Make Money with Data Entry 98
17. Make Money with Captioning Companies 101
18. Making Money With Rideshare Companies 104
19. Get Paid to Run Errands 108

20. Make Money as a Search Engine Evaluator 113

21. Get Paid to Take Surveys 118

22. Making Money from Selling Stuff 121

23. Making Money by Drop-Shipping 127

24. Winning with Amazon's FBA (Fulfillment by Amazon) Program 130

25. How To Make Money Selling Children's Used Clothing 133

26. Selling Books for Cash 135

27. Get Paid to Tutor Online 139

28. Making Money with Creativity 143

29. Sell Your Artwork for Cash 148

30. Website Flipping For Cash 151

31. Sell Your Crafts for Cash 155

32. Mystery Shopping for Cash 157

33. Make Money as a Movie Trailer Checker 166

34. Make Money by Merchandising 171

35. Making Money as a Babysitter 175

36. Make Money Pet Sitting 178

37. Make Money with Clinical Trials 184

38. Make Money as a Mock Juror 188

39. Make Money as a Weight Loss Coach 194

40. Make It Happen! 198

Bonus 199

About the Author 211

Acknowledgments

This book is dedicated to:

My loving husband and best friend, Delanza Shun-tay Carter, for encouraging me to write this book, for being supportive when I wanted to give up, and for his innate ability to occupy the kids with various activities so I could complete this book.

My daughter, Kristin Carter, and my sons, Shaun Carter and Daniel Carter, for listening as I read my drafts out loud, offering great advice, being willing to eat breakfast for dinner, and encouraging me to "get that book done" so we could do something fun!

My mom, Christina Tarr, who has always offered unwavering love and support, for helping out in every way possible to make my writing dreams a reality and for encouraging my writing efforts (from my very first story about a sick little girl named Nan who stayed home from school to the crafting of this book many years later).

My father, Lavon Tarr, for loving me, being a great dad, and not complaining when Mom came over.

My grandmother, Fannie Lee Richardson, for her incredible strength, consistent faith, and positive attitude while going through her own medical challenge and emerging victorious.

My mother-in-law, Michelle Carter, for unselfishly making delicious meals and treats for the family; and my father-in-law, Barney Lee Carter, for picking up the kiddos; and to both of them for always being willing to help out in a pinch to accommodate my writing time.

My best friend, Angela Whitaker-Payton (Moinks); my adopted mom, Darlene Norem-Smith (Mama D); my sister, Dana B. Robinson; Aunt Barbara Rhodes; Aunt Patricia J. Ray (Patty Cake); cousins Alison Turner, Lucy Beal, and Chanda Taylor-Conrad; adopted grandmom, Gladys Crump; and all my other amazing family members and friends (not mentioned here) who encouraged me to write my book and to never give up on my dream of helping others!

My researchers, motivators, idea generators, and best writing buddies, Christy Mossburg and Geradina Tomacruz; my editors, Amy Shelby, Jillian Karger, and Denise Barker; my proofreader, Meredith Dunn; and my graphic designer, Alex, for designing my dynamic eBook cover. Without your assistance, this book would not have been possible.

Finally, and most importantly, I would like to give a heartfelt thanks to all the active-income seekers reading this book. I understand that obtaining active income isn't easy and takes skills, effort, commitment, and perseverance. However, if you're willing to put in the work, you will surely reap the benefits of your efforts. I applaud you for taking the first step toward making your financial dreams a reality. You can do this! I've got faith in you!

Introduction

Let's be honest. Most Americans are living from paycheck to paycheck and are one step away from walking off a financial cliff. Life certainly isn't easy, and financial challenges throw us for a loop every time. For instance, a medical emergency, loss of your main job (for yourself or your spouse), legal woes, a wrong business decision (who knew that investing in Beanie Babies wouldn't make you rich?), or some other minor or major catastrophe, and suddenly you're pushed off the edge into financial purgatory. Bill collectors harass you. You feel stressed. Debts mount, and you feel totally out of control.

As much as we don't like to admit, talk, or think about it, these financial difficulties happen, and they happen to most of us.

Based on a federal survey done in 2013, a whopping 47% of middle-class-income-earning families cannot afford a mere $400 emergency. Now $400 may not seem like a lot, but, when you don't have it, it seems like more than a million dollars. Even more painful is that we live in the land of opportunities, but must people are experiencing "financial impotency" every day. Their income opportunities seem limited, and their minds are filled with worry, panic, and fear. Any glimmer of hope they had was smoked out with financial problems.

The good news is that you can stop this vicious cycle right now. You no longer have to experience financial stress anymore. You can take control of your life and your financial situation one active income stream at a time. You can dig yourself out of debt, restore peace of mind, establish prosperity streams, and create the life you dreamed—today!

It doesn't matter where you are now or how deep in financial trouble you feel; what matters is your commitment to changing your situation for the best. Opportunities are all around you. You just need to see them before you can work on them.

Amazingly you don't have to sweat blood and tears to make this money. You don't need to work nine hours a day, seven days a week. You don't have to become an employee in a traditional brick-and-mortar office and deal with coworkers, bosses, and all that jazz (unless you so choose). In fact, many active-income seekers I know work three to four hours a day or less, five days a week or less, and can generate over $2,000 a month in their spare time.

These intelligent individuals are living their lives to the fullest. They can work when they please, rest when they need to, and even be lazy if the mood strikes them. And they still make a nice full-time or supplemental income. Sounds like the life, doesn't it?

I've got to be honest with you though. Although I tend to be lazy and love lazy people who work smart, this plan will require a bit of work. It is not some pussyfoot plan for wimps. It is a pull-up-your-sleeves-and-get-busy plan for people not afraid to work hard (when they work) to reap the benefits in the long haul.

You must do a little soul searching. You'll need the right mind-set. You should know your talents and skills, and then choose opportunities that monetize those unique gifts. You'll apply for opportunities and work them in a systematic method. You may hit gold with one active income stream or you may need two, five, or more. I don't know, but we'll have fun figuring it out.

This plan will work for anyone who follows it. However, you must follow the plan for real results.

"Yeah, right," you may say. "I've heard it all before."

I hear you, and I can affirm that this is not a scam, and I am not filling you with hope only to let you down. I know about scams. Heck, I've been a victim of a few, and I never want you to experience any of that. On a positive note, I've also made hundreds of thousands of dollars on the Internet too. I've created several successful online ventures and freelanced for over seventeen years. I've used creativity, tenacity, and perseverance to make money and want to share my knowledge with you.

Each opportunity listed herein will be broken down into specific categories based on specific skill sets. I'll provide you with several legitimate sites for various skills. This way, you'll find methods that you can use right away to make fast cash.

Sound good? You bet it does.

Let's get started!

Active Income Streams

1. Your Success Mind-Set

Before we even delve into actual active income methods, get your mind all set for success. I want you chanting, "I believe I can earn. I believe I can attract money to my bank account. I think about it every night and day. I'm going to use my skills and make that cash. I believe I can earn."

To attract extra income, you must truly believe that you can improve your financial situation with more active income streams. Believe that you can manifest the income that you and your family need. Be confident and secure in your abilities, and then get busy doing what you need to do.

You must believe in you. Now, most people believe that seeing is believing. However, I truly believe that "once you believe it, you will see it." That is, once you believe that you're destined to succeed, you can't lose. You're destined to win.

Because prosperity begins in your mind, you must set your mind to be geared toward success. Once you believe that prosperity is coming to you, you'll be more likely to do the things you need to do to make your financial dreams a reality. Magically you'll meet the right people, see creative opportunities when none appeared previously, get hired for projects and opportunities (or create your own), and experience the magic.

When you're focused on winning and success, you can't help but succeed. If you're filled with doubt and worry, put aside those feelings right now. Make a commitment to succeed. Repeat after me: "I have the power to succeed, and nothing will stand in my way. I am committed to doing everything I must do to achieve my goals—one day at a time."

Remember that your current financial experience is only a temporary situation and is not indicative of your future outcome. You can change the direction of your finances any time you want. You have the power, the skills, and will soon have the know-how.

You are special, unique, and qualified. Companies around the world are looking for freelancers like you. They want to utilize your skills and are willing to pay you for your time.

Now, this might sound silly, but it really works if you're open and receptive. It is called the power of visualization, and I want you to use it to manifest opportunities. I've used this method hundreds of times, and it always works for me.

By visualizing the amount of money you need in your bank account or wallet, you open the floodgates for it to appear. Close your eyes and think about it. What does it feel like to have adequate income? How do you feel when you hold it in your hands or open your bank statement to see it in your account? Do you feel peaceful and content? Do you feel less stressed and more at ease? (**Note**: If you have trouble with this method, go buy some fake money, put it in your wallet, and imagine it is real.) Truly take these visualizations seriously and keep them implanted in your mind whenever times get tough.

Next, it's time to be more positive. Stop talking and focusing on what's lacking, and steer clear of naysayers who can't believe that you can actually add to your income streams as discussed in this book, thereby improving your financial picture. Although it is fine to let others know that you're open to active income opportunities, keep any financial challenges to yourself and never exclaim how no opportunities are available. Don't talk about the bad job market and don't focus on lack. Instead say, "My perfect opportunity is flowing to me right now. I will make the money I need, and I'll do it now."

Get serious. I want you to make a commitment to do what you must do to make the money flow to you. After all, you can't expect to sit on your butt all day long, practicing affirmations and visualizations, and then do nothing, yet expect the money to come to you. Instead, you must do those things that give you the proper mind-set and then take steps doing something to make your dreams a reality. You must apply for opportunities, put yourself in the right places, and do the work to reap the benefits of your positive thoughts and related actions.

Stellar Résumés and All That Jazz

Now, before you start applying for opportunities all willy-nilly, you need a stellar résumé in hand. A stellar résumé is not only a document to help present your unique background and skills to a potential employer, but it is an opportunity to outshine the competition and make an awesome first impression right away. Therefore, you can't simply slap down some job descriptions and hope for the best. Nope. You've got to really put time and effort into drafting your stellar résumé.

When you're putting your incredible résumé together, you'll either craft a chronological, functional, combined, or targeted résumé. The format that you'll use will depend on the type of position you are seeking. Here's a breakdown of styles:

- Chronological résumés are the most common types. This résumé format basically lists your work history in chronological order, starting with the most recent job first. Most employers prefer this type of résumé because it gives a quick look at your job history. Typically you are advised to use this format if you have a solid work history with no lapses between employment.

- Functional résumés focus on your skills and experience first, instead of your past work history. With this type, your work history is listed secondary to your skills, and you should use this format if you have had lapses in employment or are in the middle of a career change. For instance, if you've previously worked in the educational field as a teaching assistant but now want to work as an Uber driver, you can use this résumé format. This type is also used if you have a limited work history.

- Combined résumés feature both your skills and your experience in chronological order. This résumé can be tailored to the job you are applying for and is typically used to demonstrate your skill mastery or to highlight specialized professional or work experience.

- Targeted résumés are customizable, depending on the position for whichyou are applying. Everything can be used to mirror the requirements for this job you are applying for, from your education to your experience. This is the most time-consuming format. Highlight the experiences and skills that pertain to the position for which you are applying.

Now that you have a better understanding of the types of résumés, here are some additional tips to make your stellar résumé even better.

- Unless you're applying for an executive level position, your résumé should be limited to one page (8.5" x 11" sheet of paper) so use the space wisely.

- Keep the font for your name between 12 to 14 pts, and the font in the body of the résumé between 10 to 11 pts. If you should need extra space, you can always narrow the margins.

- Avoid cliché words. Use action words and show your personality when writing your résumé. Use bullet points to highlight the main parts.

- Only include important information. Explain your skills and qualifications so employers clearly see why you're the perfect candidate.

- Another important thing to remember when creating your résumé is to spell-check your document before you email or print it.

- Understand the position you are applying for, the skills required, and tailor your résumé specifically for that position.

- Backup your qualities and strengths with real-life examples of professional experience.

- Use the right keywords, effective titles, and bullet points.

- Always list your most important information first, especially any achievements or specialized training/certification.

- Be positive, honest, and focused on presenting information in a clear manner.

- Proofread the résumé twice and ask several other people (preferably ones familiar with the industry where you're applying) to proofread your résumé as well.

When the employer first receives your résumé, chances are they will skim through it without actually reading it—looking for things that pop out at them, either work experience, skills, or educational background. Once something grabs their attention, they will then take the time to actually read through your résumé before deciding whether to set up an interview.

Let's Get Cracking

Hopefully you're fired up and motivated to succeed, armed with your stellar résumé, and ready to grab for those opportunities and to make your vision come true. Let's take that power and energy, and move into the real meat of the book—the actual strategies to help you make moola today!

2. Usability Testing

If you're like me or other people you know, you've probably been frustrated by ugly websites or even felt like throwing your computer out the window when a website froze or stopped working. You may have even clicked and clicked on a link, growing frustrated when nothing happened. Or you may have silently cursed the website designer when the website font was so small that you could barely read it or the site was just too difficult to navigate. And, if the website's content was long, boring, or confusing, you probably got frustrated as well and clicked away from such sites.

Well, a minor annoyance for you, as the visitor of the site, equates to a huge liability for website owners. A faulty website can mean lost sales and/or subscribers, and can seriously damage their business.

To prevent this from happening, businesses invest a great deal of money into what's called "usability testing." Website usability is comprised of learnability, memorability, efficiency, satisfaction, and errors.

- <u>Learnability</u> is how easy it is for a new user to accomplish tasks the first time they visit a website.

- <u>Memorability</u> is when someone returns to a website and can navigate it easily, even after they haven't used it for a period of time.

- <u>Efficiency</u> is how quickly users can complete tasks on a site after getting familiar with its use.

- <u>Satisfaction</u> is whether users enjoy the design of a site.

- <u>Errors</u> refer to the number of errors users make when they use a site, the severity of the errors, and how easy to recover from them.

To test usability, businesses pay people to visit their site, navigate their way through the different pages, test the website's functionality, and then report back on their experiences. The businesses take that feedback, use it to fix problems and bugs, and to improve the experience of their website's users.

The businesses hire a service to manage all their usability testing for them, and those services hire testers to do the testing. And this is where you start generating a nice little side income.

The entire process of testing a website and providing feedback based on a set of instructions generally takes from ten to twenty minutes. The average pay per test is around $10, but you can earn more for specific types of tests.

And, if you do the math, you're getting paid at least $30 an hour, which isn't bad pay for playing on a website for ten minutes, then finally voicing years of frustration with faulty websites.

The first step toward becoming a tester is signing up with the different testing companies. Quite a few of them are out there, and some are better than others. Five of the top sites are listed below.

Once you register with these testing companies, you will start receiving testing requests based on your profile and demographics.

When you receive testing requests, it's very important that you respond to them right away. These companies all operate on a first-come, first-served basis so you must jump on the opportunities quickly.

Now let's get to those user testing sites to help you collect a nice pile of side cash with relatively little effort.

Usability Testing Site #1 – UserTesting

UserTesting, the most active usability testing company on this list, was founded in 2008, and allows webmasters and developers to hire people from within the United States, United Kingdom, Canada, Australia, and India to review their media. UserTesting will screen its users carefully to ensure they can articulate their thoughts and experiences effectively. You don't have to be a usability expert to get hired. In fact, hiring nonexperts is what makes their testers so valuable. They are like you, me, and any other user who may engage with the client's digital media.

How It Works

You visit a website or app, then you complete a set of tasks while speaking your thoughts out loud. A test consists of a twenty-minute recording and answers to four follow-up written questions.

What It Pays

Testers are paid $10 for each completed test.

When You Get Paid

Payments are made daily through PayPal for jobs completed seven days earlier.

Where to Sign Up: https://www.usertesting.com/be-a-user-tester

The application process is very simple. Just complete a short sample test and fill out some basic demographic information. Once you are approved, you can start taking real tests.

Equipment

You can use either a PC or Mac that meets these requirements:

PC

- Operating system: Windows XP or higher.
- Memory: At least 1 GB of total RAM and 0.5 GB of available RAM
- Free disk space: At least 5 GB of free disk space.
- Browser: Internet Explorer 8 or higher, Firefox 3.5 or higher, Safari 4 or higher, or Chrome.

Mac

- Operating system: OS X 10.7 or higher.

- Memory: At least 1 GB of total RAM and 0.5 GB of available RAM.
- Free disk space: At least 5 GB of free disk space.
- Browser: Internet Explorer 8 or higher, Firefox 3.5 or higher, Safari 4 or higher, or Chrome.

For mobile tests, you need an Android or iOS mobile phone or tablet. Sign up first to be a desktop tester, and then you can add mobile testing.

For mobile tests, your device must meet these requirements:

iOS

- Operating system: iOS 8 or higher.
- Memory: At least 400 MB of free space.

Android

- Operating system: Android 4.0 or higher.
- Memory: At least 400 MB of free space.

For either sort of test you will need a functioning microphone. Also download the screen recorder to your computer when you apply to become a tester.

Usability Testing Site #2 – TryMyUI

TryMyUI was founded in 2009 and follows a similar setup to other usability companies. Developers and webmasters submit their websites, and, if they choose you, they will send questions or tasks they would like you to answer or perform. You record yourself doing all these things with a screen recorder provided by TryMyUI for about twenty minutes and then the information is submitted to the client.

Equipment

All you need is a computer with an Internet connection and a microphone.

How It Works

Fill out a brief form and wait to be chosen to begin testing.

Use the test website exactly as you would in a real-life situation, and voice your thoughts and frustrations out loud so the site developers can understand your experience and others' like yours.

Each test consists of a video featuring your screen and voice as you use a website or app, plus your written responses to a short wrap-up survey. A typical test lasts approximately twenty minutes.

What It Pays

You will be paid $10 for each test you take.

When You Get Paid

The site sends payments every Friday through PayPal. Tests are cleared for payment after review and acceptance by the site's graders.

Where to Sign Up: http://www.trymyui.com/worker/signup

Usability Testing Site #3 – UserFeel.com

UserFeel is a remote usability testing service founded in 2010. They have a multilingual network of users all over the world and are used by web developers, designers, entrepreneurs, marketers, and more.

When a usability test is requested (that meets your specific profile and the client's needs), you'll receive the client's instructions as to what they'd like you to do. You'll then video record (with their proprietary software) the entire viewing process. This way, the client can have a clearer understanding of the entire process. By speaking into your microphone and explaining what you're doing and why, they can better understand if anything impresses or confuses you, see where you navigate and why, and more.

Equipment

For these tests you will just need a computer with an Internet connection and a microphone.

How It Works

First, you register on UserFeel and take a sample test to show that you can speak your thoughts into the microphone and that you do have a microphone of your own. Based on this sample test, you'll get the first rating to determine if—and how often—you'll get to do usability tests.

When you perform tests, remember to speak your thoughts into the microphone, say what confuses you and what attracts your attention.

Explain what and why you do what you do on the site. Propose something that would help you perform the required task. Provide useful comments. Perform the required tasks according to the test scenario. Speak loudly and clearly on the microphone. Thoroughly answer the questions in writing at the end of the test.

What It Pays

For each test you conduct after the initial sample test, you get paid $10. Most active testers that provide useful feedback to clients make about $100–$200 a month.

When You Get Paid

At the end of each week, via PayPal.

Where to Sign Up:

http://www.userfeel.com/index.php?option=com_userfeel&view=register&layout=testers&Itemid=8

Usability Testing Site #4 – StartUpLift

StartUpLift was founded in 2010 specifically to help entrepreneurs grow their businesses. It caters to companies looking for specialized usability tasks that they can employ to improve their overall brand awareness.

Active Income Streams

Equipment

You must be connected to the Internet and have a web browser. At times when customers mention a specific requirement (e.g., use Firefox only), you will be notified of such.

How It Works

Use a valid PayPal address during registration; you do not need to enter your PayPal address separately.

Startups provide their website URL and assign tasks that they would like you to perform/complete and also to provide written responses. Any available opportunity will be listed on your Opportunities Dashboard after you sign in.

Once you've selected an opportunity, you visit the website, complete assigned tasks, share your thoughts, and provide insightful written responses. You must be registered and logged in when you provide feedback in order to be considered for an award and payment.

What It Pays

You will be paid $5 for every feedback accepted.

When You Get Paid

Cash awards are transferred to PayPal accounts every week on Monday.

Where to Sign Up: http://startuplift.com/wp-login.php?action=register

Usability Testing Site #5 – Usability Hub

UsabilityHub is a usability testing site founded in 2008. This site mainly targets individuals who have a few minutes here and there to share their knowledge with designers and clients who need advice from a wide range of individuals.

Equipment

You must be connected to the Internet and have a web browser. If you want to use their add-on notification, you'll need Firefox.

How It Works

Fill out a profile with your preferences. You'll then be eligible for usability tests based on your profile and what the client is seeking.

With this site, bookmark it and visit it often so you can check for tests, or leave their notification tool open in one tab so you can be notified if a test (which you qualify for) is available. You'll then get a beep when a test is added.

Unlike other sites, UsabilityHub doesn't provide invitations for projects. I'm guessing it is because they have a lot of reviewers, and the tests get snatched up quickly. Thus check in often so you don't miss out on any moneymaking opportunities.

From the webmaster or developer side of things, UsabilityHub has some really quick tests to choose from that typically take thirty seconds to a few minutes to complete. Tasks include reviewing a site for thirty seconds or more and then reporting what you remember; reviewing two sites and then choosing your preferred design; answering questions about a website's navigation; and more.

Once your responses are submitted to the client, the client reviews them and then must be approved by the review team. You will be paid once you reach the $20 payment threshold for approved responses.

What It Pays

The pay rate for UsabilityHub is very unique. You earn credits instead of dollars. Each credit is worth $0.10, and most tests pay one credit, on average, for one minute in length. Usability claims that you can make

$6–$10 per hour taking tests, but this will vary, depending on the number of tests. There have been times when I've completed five tests in a row and days when I received none. Either way, you must reach two hundred credits before you can request a PayPal payout.

When It Pays

You are paid when you request payment, and it typically takes a day or two for the review team to review past responses and for payment to be sent via PayPal.

Where to Sign Up: https://usabilityhub.com/testers

3. Writing Content for Cash

Assuming you have above-average writing skills, you can make a lot of money writing articles and other web content, like press releases, eBooks, short reports, web content, and business and marketing plans. Plus the good news is that you need not be the next William Shakespeare or Edgar Allen Poe to make a decent living as a writer. The average part-time writer works between three to five hours a day and can set his/her own schedules. They typically work when they're able. Most writers make about $25 per hour and work for a variety of different clients, including Fortune 500s, nonprofits, magazines, small businesses and presses, larger publishing companies or newspapers. The possibilities are endless, as quality content is needed in every sector.

If you don't have a lot of writing experience and/or are unsure of your skills, you can improve them with online courses. In addition, you can even learn how to writer faster to maximize your income. Here are some great courses for you to check out:

1. CollegeDegree.com – This site has a list of over fifty open courseware writing classes from leading universities, and there is no charge for the courses.

2. International Webmasters Association – This site offers a six-week course where you can learn effective techniques in writing. There are no prerequisites and no requirements. There is a charge of $100.

3. Media Bistro – Many courses are available on this site to enhance your writing. You pick and choose which course you would like to take. There is a fee for the courses on this site.

Once you're more confident in your skills, you can find many opportunities for paid work—in fact, even some companies whose primary business model is to match writers with clients. Many people refer to these organizations as "content farms," but, if you're a fast writer who produces quality work, you can milk those "content farms" and get full off the cream that the milk provides—moola, *ka-ching*, baby. For instance, Textbroker and HireWriters are two popular sites that have a consistent flow of writing projects available.

Content Writing Site #1 – Textbroker

Textbroker is a site that matches freelancers with clients who need help with copy. Projects range from articles to press releases to short reports. They also have a proofreading option as well.

How It Works

To get hired as an independent contractor, submit a writing sample to obtain your rating and access to paid assignments. Rates vary depending on various factors, For instance, five-star writers are paid higher rates than two-star writers. However, if a client contacts you directly via Textbroker's private message system, you can set your own rates. Also, if you're chosen for a team, the rates could be higher, depending on the client's budget.

Writer ratings range from two to five and are based on your previously approved articles and samples. These include spelling, grammar, punctuation, style, argument strength, whether the article has too much filler material, and so on. Ratings are very important because writers can only see and accept assignments for their current rating or any lower ratings. For instance, a four-star writer can see four-, three-, and two-level assignments, while a two-star writer can only see two-level assignments, and a five-star writer can see all levels.

After your Textbroker profile is finished, complete your extended author profile. An author profile includes your writing experience, languages you speak, hobbies and interests, countries you've visited, and the like.

Once your profile is completed and you're ranked, you start by choosing a writing project within your rating level.

After you submit your content, your client will either ask for a revision or decline/accept the article. They can then rate it with one to five stars and leave a comment about the quality of the content. You are only paid for accepted content.

At Textbroker you can be promoted or demoted at any time. So, even if you start at a four-star level, you may get demoted to a two if the quality of your work decreases. By the same token, you could start off at a two and end up as a five-star writer.

Each completed article receives a rating from the client (based on stars), and clients can leave specific comments. Then the article receives a separate rating from a Textbroker review expert that doesn't affect your pay but affects your overall rating. For instance, your client could approve the article and you'd be paid, but you could still get a rating of three from the review team.

What It Pays

You are paid per word, and the pay varies depending on your rating. The higher the rating, the more money you make. For instance, a four-star writer completing a four-hundred-word article would receive $5.60, whereas a three-star writer would receive $4.50 for the same word count.

When It Pays

You can request payment after you've passed the $10 threshold. The request must be received by 11:59 p.m. on Thursday to be paid on Friday via PayPal. If you miss the deadline, it will be paid the following week.

Where to Sign Up: Http://www.textbroker.com

Content Writing Site #2 – HireWriters.com

HireWriters is a website currently looking for freelance writers to match with their pool of paying clients. Join HireWriters for free. This company welcomes bilingual writers but requests that English be the writer's first language. They're currently recruiting writers from the United States of America, Canada, United Kingdom, New Zealand, Singapore, and Australia. HireWriters also requires that writers have good writing skills (correct grammar, punctuation, etc.).

How It Works

When writers initially start, they are typically ranked by experience and paid accordingly, as follows:

- **Beginner writer** – Everyone starts off as a beginner and moves his/her way up based on quality of work, timeliness, and client reviews.

- **General writer** – These writers have at least three reviews with four stars or higher and can keep their late-turn-in percentage at 30% or lower.

- **Skilled writer** – A skilled writer needs seven reviews and a 4.1 rating or higher. They must also not turn in work late over 23% of the time.

- **Expert writer** – An expert writer needs fourteen reviews with a 4.6 or higher rating, and they can't be late more than 12% of the time.

One positive thing about this site is that you are in control of how much you work and earn. If you see an article you want, pick it up. If you don't, leave it there for someone else to choose.

To get started on HireWriters, create a stellar profile accentuating your skills, and add a writing sample and biography. You'll then search for suitable opportunities, depending on your rank.

What It Pays

The pay rates at HireWriters vary but their site says that, if you're just starting off and write an article, you could earn $2.25. However, an expert article could earn $10.66. So your goal should be to increase your ranking as soon as possible. Clients may also offer a bonus if very satisfied with your work.

When It Pays

Once you have $10 in your account, you are paid automatically via PayPal. No request for payment is needed.

Advanced tips to increase your income at HireWriters:

1. Pay special attention to the project deadlines and customer ratings. Only accept projects that you can realistically finish.

Unlike some companies, HireWriters deducts money from your account when you miss a deadline. Missed deadlines not only affect your rating but they'll also prohibit you from getting higher paid assignments.

2. Evaluate clients' acceptance rates and accept projects from customers who have a higher rating. They'll be more likely to approve your articles, assuming they're well-written and unique.

3. Never plagiarize and always exceed client expectations. They are paying for original work so properly cite any sources and only submit your best work. Your reputation as a writer depends on it.

Where to Sign Up: http://www.HireWriters.com

In addition to Textbroker and HireWriters, some sites that also hire writers are:

1. The Content Authority – This writing opportunity works on tiers. The better the content, the better the pay. The pay is somewhat low at the start. A four-hundred-word article pays only a couple dollars. To be considered for a writing position here, you must write formal articles at a high school level, do accurate research, follow instructions, meet deadlines, and need a PayPal account.

2. Writer's Domain – Writers are given keywords and then are asked to write about them. The pay scale is $3 for 250–300 words, with a possible bonus of $0.30 for high ratings. They pay monthly on the fifth. After you apply to be a writer, you will receive an email with more information. There is a video to watch, sample writings to review, and a thirty-question test to take.

3. Purecontent – This site accepts writers from all over the world, as long as English is their first language. It offers opportunities to write industry news, blog posts, articles, infographs, and editorials. Pay starts at $3.30 per 250 words

and goes up from there. They pay once a month for the previous month's work. After applying here, you will have two weeks to complete the packet sent to you via email.

4. Article Document – As a writer starting out here, you will complete blogging assignments. As you progress through the levels, you can make your way to journalist assignments. Pay is determined on the quality and popularity of the article. The application process is pretty simple. Once you have supplied them with all the information they request and set up your account, you may start writing.

5. Ghost Bloggers – The writing projects posted here are keyword-based. You will not receive credit for your work, and they'll publish the work in their name. Pay is around $3.50 per one hundred words.

Now that you have a better idea of the opportunities available to you, hopefully you'll consider this active income stream.

Here are some advanced writing tips to help you get the most of these writing opportunities:

1. **Write like you're talking to someone else.** You will find that the words come much easier if you simply write as though you are talking to an individual about the different points of a specific topic. In fact, when you write like this, it often makes your article easier to read too. Rather than trying to use words that make your article seem pompous, use words that anyone from a fifth-grade level and above could comprehend.

2. **Use the 80/20 method.** With this method, you spend about 80% of your time researching and collecting information about the topic. Then you spend the remaining 20% of your time writing the article. This makes writing the article much easier, as you've already gotten the resources you need, and you're informed and ready to go.

3. **Stick to what you know.** Write articles about topics you're already familiar with or are happy to research. If you're writing articles about stuff you know already, you can write them more efficiently. For instance, you might have nursing experience.

Break down this knowledge into different articles, such as "How to Build an Insulated Doghouse to Avoid Frostbite or Hypothermia in Your Pet" or "How to Know When It's Time for an Emergency Room Visit." By writing about topics you already are familiar with, you can get them done faster.

4. **Focus on your craft.** Devote an adequate amount of time to writing content. You can even use the Pomodoro Technique. Francesco Cirillo developed this routine in the late 1980s. Use a timer to break down work intervals into twenty-five-minute increments. This is how the Pomodoro Technique works:

   1. Decide what task needs to be done.

   2. Set a timer.

   3. Work until the timer dings.

   4. Afterward, place a checkmark on a piece of paper.

   5. If you have less than four checkmarks at this time, take a break for three to five minutes and go back to step 1.

   6. If you have four checkmarks, take a longer break (fifteen to thirty minutes long), and then reset the checkmarks and return to step 1.

In conclusion, when you use these methods to find a freelance writing gig, you can make a nice chunk of change writing articles for clients. Plus you'll help others who don't have the time or skills to write articles themselves. A true win-win situation, right?

Where to Sign Up:

The Content Authority - http://thecontentauthority.com/

Article Document - https://www.articledocument.com/

Writer's Domain - https://www.writersdomain.net/

Purecontent - http://www.purecontent.com/

Ghost Bloggers - http://www.ghostbloggers.net/

4. Make Money Writing Reviews and Blogging (Sponsored Posts)

Businesses understand that good publicity is the difference between a successful business and an unsuccessful one. As such, they are willing to pay good money for advertising to increase their brand awareness. What you may not know is that many of these companies hire bloggers to promote their products and services through sponsored posts. With sponsored posts, you basically discuss a product or service and state whether you would recommend it.

Combining paid advertising with sponsored posts is another great way for bloggers to make more money. Paid blogging enables bloggers to sometimes earn as much as $500–$2,000 per month or more from writing sponsored posts. The greater your traffic, the more likely your readers are to buy the advertised item, and the more money you make.

Business blogging has increased by 31% in the last three years, and there is a very simple reason why. Consumers are tired of hearing hard-sell in-your-face ads that they have learned to zone out. However, they need information so they turn to experts for recommendations, solutions, and leads. According to recent research from the Californian research firm Gleanster, business blogs serve two main purposes:

1. They provide information.

2. They keep products or services in the limelight so consumers don't forget about them when they finally decide to make a purchase.

At the rate businesses are turning to blogging, experts predict that the current number of bloggers will have more to write about as the demand rises. Establishing a reputation as a reliable blogger now will help you get a piece of that market which is expected to explode by 2020. Why 2020? Professionals believe that, by then, most sales will not involve person-to-person contact, and consumers will not be checking a product's website but rather its reviews and feedback first before adding or scratching it off their shopping list.

Advanced tips to get paid review assignments for paid review sites:

- According to Federal Trade Commission (FTC) regulations, you must include a disclaimer if the post was paid for, to remain in compliance with consumer protection laws. This is to uphold its truth-in-advertising principles.

- Make sure your blog has a unique design, is not too template-dictated, and is easy to navigate. Also steer clear of profanity and grammatical errors.

- Ensure that your blog posts are well-written and tell a creative story that draws in the readers and keeps them wanting more. The posts need a marketing edge but should not be overly promotional.

- Have a catchy title to draw in the readers—but ensure the title is not too long because the attention span of today's online users is a few seconds, at most.

- Make it easy to read the review by using bullet points, short paragraphs, and bold text for emphasis.

- Select the right keywords for the blog so it can get ranked and appear high on an Internet search.

Below we will discuss some of the companies that pay for product reviews.

Sponsored Posts #1 – Sponsored Reviews

Sponsored Reviews is a marketplace for purchasing and selling sponsored reviews on your blog. Here are the things you need to qualify for writing with this site:

- A blog at least three months old and with at least ten high-quality posts published.

- A blog indexed in all the major search engines.
- A blog containing only original content.
- A blog with a good rating gives you a better chance of acceptance.
- An active PayPal account.

Once you have been accepted, you can write paid reviews for advertisers available on the Sponsored Reviews website. Some advertisers will browse through the blogs listed and offer moneymaking opportunities. You should only accept those offers that relate to your blog readers. Advertisers are looking for feedback and honest reviews about their products.

There is also a bidding system. You can bid on available advertising opportunities. If your bid is accepted, you will then have one week to write your review/blog post for that advertiser.

You will earn 50% of the fee. So, if you write a review worth $100, you will earn $50 and the other $50 goes to Sponsored Reviews. Payments will be automatically sent to you every two weeks via PayPal.

There is also an affiliate program, where you can earn up to $175 per advertiser. If you refer a new blogger to this program, you will earn $75.

Where to Sign Up: http://www.sponsoredreviews.com/

Sponsored Posts #2 – Review Stream

Review Stream is a website looking for people to do product reviews as listed on their website. They have products in categories from baby items to video games. If you have used the product, you are qualified to write a review. The review needs to be written in your own words. Any review written for this site cannot be used to review the same item on another site. The review should be at least five hundred words. The rate they pay for a review varies from day to day with the average range being $7–$8. You will not be paid for a review unless it is accepted by Review Stream. They pay once a month through PayPal.

They also have other ways of making money on your reviews. If you get positive votes on your review from other readers, you will receive $10 for every vote. You can also earn $10 for replying to questions from other readers, so, if you know the answer to the unanswered questions, answer them. There is also a referral program. If you refer a person to write reviews, you will earn 2% of their earnings.

Where to Sign Up: Review Stream - http://www.reviewstream.com/

Sponsored Posts #3 – Software Judge

Software Judge is a website that pays users for reviews on software listed on the Software Judge site. Choose one you would like to write a review on. You are limited to writing only three reviews per day. The reviews you write about the software should be honest and constructive. They will pay up to $50 for a review. The prices will vary, depending on the type of software it is.

There are three ways to be paid:

1. Digital freebies, such as free games and free registration keys.

2. Cash—paid through Western Union once you have at least $200 in your account.

3. Software exchange. You need at least $20 in your account to download the listed available software.

Where to Sign Up: http://www.softwarejudge.com

5. Make Money with Forum-Posting Companies

Do you enjoy visiting forums? Do you participate in several forums, or are you a lurker? Either way, forum owners need active forum members. The more active a forum is, the more likely people will contribute and add informative posts. The more posts, the "stickier" the site becomes, and the more others will visit. Interestingly, companies on the net will pay you to post on their clients' forums. These companies have set up a platform where forum owners can hire posters to comment on existing posts (or create new ones) so their site grows.

In order to excel at this opportunity, you must be a good conversationalist, be interested in the forum's subject matter, and be willing to contribute your knowledge to others. Do this, and you'll not only help the forum grow but you'll be paid for your time.

When working as a forum poster, you should be as helpful as possible. Sometimes you'll run into Internet trolls and people who will throw nasty comments at you. However, you still must maintain a cool head and act professionally at all times. For those who have a gift of gab, forum posting is a great opportunity to make some steady cash.

Although each company has a different payment structure, you'll most likely make around $10 for eighty to one hundred forum posts. While $10 doesn't seem like much money, keep in mind that, if you're a fast typist (75 wpm or higher), you can crank out the required twenty-word to fifty-word responses rather quickly.

To get started, you must apply. In some instances, you'll write a few free forum posts or submit a forum post writing sample before you are accepted for paid posts. After that, however, you can earn money for every post you make.

Here are a few companies that might hire you as a forum poster:

1. Postloop - A company that pays for posts to forums and blogs. You are paid daily via PayPal, and you must have at least $5 for a payout. The writer criteria is stringent, and excellent grammar is a must. You are required to submit ten samples before earning points. Blog or forum owners can easily pay for points that can enable posts onto their own sites. Sign-up is easy and quick. Postloop is a fun way to earn some extra money doing what you may already enjoy doing.

2. Professional Forum Posters – A simple, straightforward website for earning money. To sign up is a two-step process. You must submit ten posts and threads prior to posting as part of the application process. They look for grammar, spelling, and punctuation. You can earn $0.25 per post.

3. Paid Forum Posting – Existing since 2005, this company prides itself in not just posting in forums but on creating content. In order to join, you must create seven unique posts consisting of four topics and three replies. This site pays around $0.20 per post, and you must submit for payment. This forum connects you to forum owners who will pay you for your efforts so the payment method differs according to each forum owner. Typically they use PayPal.

Other forums to consider are:

- CashFindForum.com
- EarningPalace.com
- MyLot.com

Where to Sign Up:

Post Loop - http://www.postloop.com/

Professional Forum Posters - http://proforumposters.proboards.com/

Paid Forum Posting - http://www.paidforumposting.com/content/

Cash Find Forum - http://www.cashFindforum.com

Earning Palace - http://www.earningpalace.com

My Lot - http://mylot.com

6. Freelancing for Cash (Writers, Web Designers, and Graphic Designers)

Did you know that over 472 million entrepreneurs exist worldwide and over 305 million businesses start up every single year? In addition, many business owners don't have the capital to hire part- or full-time staff members so many hire freelancers to complete everyday and specialized tasks.

In 2016, freelancing was considered one of the biggest growth hacks in enabling start-ups and small businesses to compete globally, despite their budgetary constraints. According to the *Economist*, 90% of businesses cited outsourcing as the main reason for their continued growth and also stated that outsourcing can significantly improve competitiveness and productivity from 10%–100%.

But the good news doesn't stop there for freelancers. In 2014, an independent research firm, Edelman Berland, commissioned the Freelancers Union in partnership with Elance-Upwork to evaluate more than 5,050 US working adults in *Freelancing in America: A National Survey of the New Workforce*. These workers were over the age of eighteen, with 1,720 freelancers and 3,332 non freelancers evaluated. Researchers discovered that one in every three people is a freelancer for a whopping total of fifty-three million freelancers in the United States.

To break this down further, the study found five freelancing segments, which include:

- **Independent contractors or traditional contractors**, who complete supplemental, temporary, or freelance assignments on a project-to-project basis. They make up 40% of the independent workforce.

- **Moonlighters**, who have a regular job but do freelance work on the side. Moonlighting freelancers make up 27% of the freelancing workforce.

- **Diversified workers**, who hold many active income sources. For instance, they may work both as a Lyft driver and as a work-at-home editor. These workers make up 18% of the freelancing workforce.

- **Temporary workers**, who work with a single client for a short- or medium-term project. These workers make up 10% of the freelancing workforce.

- **Freelance business owners**, who own freelance businesses. These business owners make up 5% of the freelancing workforce.

If you're interested in joining this growing workforce as one of the above freelancers, many companies, like Upwork, match prospective clients with qualified freelancers.

Here are a few to check out:

Freelance Bidding Site #1 – Upwork

Upwork used to be known as the highly successful Elance-oDesk, a merger of two of the largest freelance websites that pioneered this type of online income opportunity.

Now they are a combined force that connects freelance workers—like web designers, graphic designers, and writers—to employers who post thousands of projects every day. If you possess a set of skills that you'd like to put to use and to work on within your own timetable from your chosen location, then Upwork is the perfect place for you.

How It Works

To get started, sign up for free as a contractor in your chosen field. In order to be successful, you should create a stellar profile that demonstrates your skills and talents as your first step. You'll need a professional photograph, a portfolio of your work, and a short written overview of your skills. You can even record a video to be viewed by clients.

Once your profile is created, your next order of business should be to take some tests relevant to your field. If you're a writer, these would include some tests on English grammar, spelling, vocabulary, and so on. Frequently tests are used by employers to screen contractors, so take a few tests, as these will only cost you a little time in the beginning and will be extremely useful in your Upwork journey.

You now must decide on an hourly work rate. There is no standard amount, and it depends on the field in which you are working. Look up some successful freelancers in your field and figure out an average rate. If you're new to Upwork with no feedback or jobs, it would be wise to keep your rate toward the lower end of the scale at first.

After you've set up your profile and taken a few tests, you're ready to apply for projects. Upwork works through a "connects" system where two connects allow a freelancer to apply to one job. A basic free Upwork account comes with sixty connects per month, meaning you can apply for thirty jobs. This number may be a little less for newer freelancers. In order to apply for more jobs, additional connects can be bought for $1 per connect.

Freelancers with connects can apply for jobs in many different fields, such as writing, web development, design, etc. Jobs are of two types: hourly or fixed-rate. Freelancers can search newly posted jobs, apply to each with a cover letter, and answer any other questions that may be part of the job posting. You can bid a flat-fee amount or hourly rate—lower, higher, or equal to the one in the job posting.

Landing your first job is crucial, so you may want to bid very low just to increase your chances of getting a job. Think of this first job as a way to prove yourself. Once you've completed the job, the employer can end the contract and provide you with rating from one to five. A high rating (a five) will help you in getting work in the future.

Perks for Top-Rated Freelancers

Upwork also rewards the best freelancers by giving them a Top Rated status. According to the Upwork website, in order to receive this status, freelancers must possess all of the following:

- A current Job Success Score of 90% or higher.

- Maintaining a Rising Talent status or a Job Success Score of at least 90% for at least thirteen of the past sixteen weeks.

- A profile that has been filled out 100%. **Note:** People who migrated from Elance only need 90% completed.

- At least $1,000 in earnings over the past twelve months.

- Availability to accept projects now and, if not available, a date when they will be.

- An account that is not defaulted.

- Activity on the site within ninety days. This includes accepting or responding to invitations, submitting proposals, or earning income.

According to Upwork, the perks received by these top-rated freelancers include:

- A badge on your Upwork freelancer profile.

- Personalized tips to strengthen your profile.

- Premium customer support, including phone and chat.

- Exclusive invitations to submit proposals.

- An exclusive Job Digest email to make it easier for you to find attractive opportunities.

- The ability to exercise more control over your Job Success Score.

- Private access to special community forums, office hours, and citywide events.

What It Pays

Your hourly rate will depend on the amount you request in your bid. However, Upwork will deduct a fee from any payments you receive. These fees range from 5%–20%, as follows:

- 20% for the first $500 you bill a client across all contracts with them.
- 10% for total billings with a client between $500.01 and $10,000.
- 5% for total billings with a client that exceed $10,000.

Upwork also guarantees payments so you can be confident about getting paid for work you've done. For hourly contracts, Upwork has time-tracking software that monitors your activity as you track work and takes periodic screenshots. The time tracked on hourly contracts is paid out within two weeks.

Fixed-rate contracts are similarly protected; however, before getting started, ensure that the client sets up milestone payments to be released in escrow. This simply means that the client has paid an amount with Upwork which will be released in the future upon completion of work. You can transfer your earnings to your bank account.

How It Pays

Contractors are paid via PayPal or ACH bank deposit.

When It Pays

Your payment due for hourly work is available based on a weekly billing cycle, found here. Payments from fixed-price projects, bonuses, final payments, milestone payments, etc., are paid once the respective client remits payment and after five days have elapsed.

Where to Sign Up: http://www.upwork.com

Freelance Bidding Site #2 – Freelancer

Freelancer is an Australian-based company that claims to be the world's top crowdsourcing marketplace because it is available in 247 countries and has close to twenty million freelancers and employees on its roster. Just as the name suggests, Freelancer is a freelance marketplace where clients search for competent professionals and contractors to bid for jobs.

How It Works

To get started, you should sign up for a free account. Like Upwork, you'll create an exceptional profile, add your work experience, picture, and so on. When signing up, you can select twenty skills which best describe your talents. The free membership makes ten bids available to you each month to apply for jobs. Beyond this, the basic plan allows fifty bids a month, and you can add thirty skills. The standard plan enables 150 bids, and you can add up to sixty skills. Here you also must decide on an hourly rate.

On Freelancer, you'll find fixed projects, hourly projects, and contests posted as well. Contests are crowdsourced jobs where clients can view a variety of submissions from freelance contestants before choosing and paying for the one they like the most. They typically work well for production of T-shirt and website designs, logos, etc. Projects are completed only by the one chosen freelancer, awarded through the bidding process.

Taking tests on Freelancer is helpful, and, again, employers often use these tests as screening tools. However, tests on Freelancer are not paid, but you should invest in taking a few, as these are important elements of demonstrating your skills, seeming more marketable, and getting the attention of clients.

A higher rating and good feedback helps freelancers get more work. So, for a newbie, bidding low and just getting some decent feedback should be the goal for the first couple jobs. Freelancer allows you to see the project cost, as well as the average bid, so you can use this information to make a smart offer. You can apply to ten jobs but take time to read the job description for each and draft your cover letters accordingly.

With Freelancer, it's highly recommended to make use of milestones with project-based work. In this way, employers can pay in steps, and both parties are assured of recurring work and payment installments. Payments can be transferred weekly or at any other time to a bank account, Skrill, or through PayPal.

What It Pays

The amount you make depends on a variety of factors, including your skills, the projects you work on, and the field you're in. Generally, web design, app development, and graphic design will pay more than writing or editing. However, even within one field, there are different types of projects. The ones that require high-quality work will pay more and others less. You can make up to $100,000 per year once you've managed to gain some experience!

When It Pays

For project-based work, you are paid when milestones are reached, projects are completed, or contests are won. It depends on the type of project and agreement made with each client at the time of acceptance. For contests, you are paid when the client accepts your winning proposal and rights are transferred to them.

Now that we've discussed the tips of signing up for Upwork and Freelancer, here are **ten great tips** on how to win bids and get projects.

1. **Read the proposal carefully.** Ensure that you have read through the entire project description completely. One annoying thing that many bidders do is scan through without actually reading the project description. Then they suddenly realize that they're not qualified for any of the skills the client is requesting. When you bid on the project, ensure that you have all the skills needed by the client. And, if you don't, be willing to obtain them in order to exceed your client's high expectations.

2. **Don't bid with a generic proposal.** Many bidders also bid on projects using generic proposals. This is not the way to go if you want someone to trust you with his or her project. Take your time to formulate an original bid and talk directly to the

prospective client. Mention some details that you read so future clients will know that you've truly paid attention. Visit their website and make specific suggestions to help them improve some aspect of their business. This point alone can really help you win projects!

3. **Be open and willing to do more than asked.** If a client requests one writing sample, send two. If they would like you to do a paid writing sample of five hundred words, write six hundred words. Always be willing to impress a future client. This will ensure that you can meet their expectations.

4. **Keep your price fair but don't undersell yourself.** You definitely don't want to give away your work, but you want to keep your price fair and competitive as well. Check out what other bidders are bidding. Although you can go slightly higher or lower, keep it in the same range so the prospective client will feel that you're charging a fair price. However, if you feel that you're significantly more skilled than the other bidders, feel free to bid what you think is fair and tell the client why you're worth more.

5. **Include a résumé and samples with your bid.** By including a résumé and samples with your bid, the poster of the project gets a chance to see your range of abilities and skills. They can study the types of projects you've completed in the past. Link to online profiles, like LinkedIn, so they can see references. Great samples can win you bids sometimes, so be sure to choose your very best ones. If you don't currently have any samples, create some (relevant to the project you're applying for) so that you have something to show.

6. **Do something crazy.** If you're bidding against five or more candidates, do something to make yourself stand out. Include a special guarantee (like 20% off regular rates if they choose you today) or offer to give them a free article with a prepaid order or something like that. Or, if you're a web designer, and you see that the prospective client's website is in a color that should never be used or there is too much (or not enough) white space, let him know and tell him how to improve it.

7. **Communicate with prospects.** Oftentimes prospective clients will have questions to ask you and want additional information. Always state in your bid that you're willing to provide them with additional information. Tell them that you're open to a Skype or phone interview to go over project specs.

8. **Finish test projects early.** If you're given a test project, always send it in early. If you absolutely can't, tell your prospective client right away and then give them something extra for the additional time it took.

9. **Treat your clients with respect.** Always treat prospective clients with respect. Don't devalue their time with canned bids or applying for jobs you have no interest in. Instead, only apply for jobs that actually interest you and are guaranteed to showcase your strengths.

10. **Enjoy the selection process.** Don't feel bad if you aren't selected. Instead, review your proposal and figure out how to improve it next time. You can even review the winner's proposal to see why they were chosen instead of you.

Where to Sign Up: http://www.freelancer.com

7. Nonbidding Freelance Sites

If bidding on projects is not your thing, no worries. Not everyone enjoys a competitive environment, and that's okay. The good news is that several well-known companies have done away with the bidding process. With these companies, you simply choose available projects to complete based on your interests and skills. You don't have to compete with other contractors with complicated bids or time-consuming proposals.

Here are a few opportunities that might interest you:

Nonbidding Freelance Site #1 – Fancy Hands

Fancy Hands is an online company established in 2016 which offers virtual assistance for clients all over the world, handling small administrative tasks (including emails and phone calls), writing, and research tasks for clients with memberships. At Fancy Hands, you'll work with a team of virtual assistants and pick up projects on demand. They're open 24/7.

You'll see a few differences between Fancy Hands and other virtual assistant services. One of the main differences is no bidding required for tasks like on other freelance sites. Instead, it is more a first-come, first-served model.

How It Works

The tasks will be listed on the dashboard, and the virtual assistant can choose any task they would like as long as no one else has claimed it. When you're initially hired, you start off as a virtual assistant, but you eventually can become a mentor, which earns you a little more money on average.

No specific requirements are listed for becoming a Fancy Hands virtual assistant; however, you should have good communication, organizational, administrative, research, and writing skills. In addition, you'll need a working computer and Internet service, and must have access to software programs like Word or Excel.

The application process is fairly easy and consists of you taking a quiz, conducting research, or completing a task for a client. For instance, you may be asked what program opens up docx files or something similar. You'll be tested on your ability to follow directions and your knowledge of grammar. So be sure to proofread your work and answer questions carefully! Fancy Hands gets back to you rather quickly (within a week or so).

The tasks aren't really divided—except for a separate page set up for incoming-call tasks—and all are otherwise listed on the dashboard. The tasks are organized by the posting time of the customers. So the top task on the list is the one posted for the longest period of time.

Once you finish an assignment, the client rates your work with one to five stars, and your mentor must approve it before the job is closed and before you're paid.

What It Pays

With Fancy Hands, you can make around $25 per day (working only four hours a day). The revenue depends on how active you are with claiming and completing tasks. Each task typically ranges from $2–$5, so, if you work a regular 9-to-5 schedule, you can potentially earn $48 to $120 or so, depending on the type of task and its respective pay.

When It Pays

Fancy Hands pays its assistants every two weeks on Tuesdays.

How It Pays

Assistants at Fancy Hands are paid via Dwolla, an online payment system.

Additional Tips You Should Know

1. Only select projects that interest you and that you can do successfully.

2. Work quickly and effectively, and do your best. If a project takes longer than the allocated twenty minutes, let your client know and ask if they'd be willing to pay for another one to two

tasks. Once the client approves your request, your manager will be informed to credit you with another task.

Where to Sign Up: https://www.fancyhands.com/jobs

Nonbidding Freelance Site #2 – Time Etc

Time Etc is another website offering opportunities for US- and UK-based freelancers to earn money as virtual assistants. The business began in the United Kingdom and just recently entered the US market.

How It Works

Once buyers sign up, they are immediately helped by one of the website's advisors/mentors and given a list of potential workers to choose from.

Once assistants sign up, they can then post a profile and engage in a one-on-one interview with prospective clients via phone, Skype, or email. The client then works with the freelancer directly while the project manager oversees all communications. If the assistant is unsatisfied with the client or vice versa, either one can easily shift to another until you both find that perfect working relationship.

Unlike other sites, you can build a strategic partnership with your client, and they become dependent on you.

Here are some insider tips to getting hired by Time Etc:

1. Be prepared for an in-depth telephone interview by a Time Etc hiring manager. Ensure you have an updated résumé and can verify information. You will likely be asked about specific projects you've worked on and positions you've held that can easily translate to being a virtual assistant (VA). So be clear about your unique skills and don't be afraid to "sell yourself" during the interview.

2. You must have great organizational and administrative skills, and have demonstrated the ability to be a self-starter. If you have worked remotely in the past, this is even better. The

hiring manager wants to ensure that you'll exceed clients' expectations and be counted on in a pinch.

3. Time Etc administers a test assignment to prospects as the last step to getting hired. It's fairly simple but pay attention to the instructions. Read them carefully and then read them again. Because they're measuring your attention-to-detail skills, you must be able to follow these directions.

4. Time Etc starts off all its VAs with a pay of $11 an hour. You are eligible for a small raise after six months of active and satisfactory work. The number of hours you work for them is completely up to you. They will try to keep you busy as long as you show you can do the job, so let them know whenever you want to work more hours.

5. The best way to succeed at Time Etc is to do the work you're assigned in a timely manner, and stay in contact with your client and the manager who you're assisting. If you need time off, be clear and don't flake out on a customer. Instead, do your best to get the work done in a timely fashion.

How It Pays

Time Etc pays via PayPal so you'll need a valid PayPal account in order to receive payments.

When It Pays

The pay schedule for Time Etc is once a month. For example, on August 10, you will be paid for all the hours you worked in July. If you're looking to make quick cash, you need a backup plan in mind, as you could feasibly work for forty days before you get your first paycheck.

Here are a few tips for maintaining positive client relationships:

1. When you receive an assignment from Time Etc, you either accept it or deny it. Be sure that you can handle this assignment before you accept it. Manage your workload efficiently. So, if you're busy with other clients or are not interested in the offered assignment, turn it down. You will not be penalized for

doing so, and it's much better to not take it on than to disappoint a client.

2. The system is very easy to use, and your account manager will monitor all messages between you and the client, and intervene if necessary. A calendar system is set up where you indicate your unavailable dates so that they do not send you assignments on those days.

3. Have fun. Time Etc is a great place to work and has a lot to offer. Once you develop strategic partnerships with your manager and clients, you'll have a steady flow of assignments to keep you busy for a long time.

Where to Sign Up:
http://timeetc.co.uk/wdt/virtual_assistant/portal/apply_now

Nonbidding Freelance Site #3 – Fiverr

Fiverr is a really interesting company created in 2009 and launched in 2010. Fiverr's initial hook was to give creative individuals a place to earn income outside of a traditional job and to give buyers a place to easily obtain inexpensive services for $5. Fiverr has grown exponentially since it was founded and now boasts over two million "gigs" available (a "gig" is simply a service listed on the site). Although gigs all start at $5 (as the name implies), the prices for add-on services can reach as high as $500. The amount a seller can charge depends on their Fiverr level, which is determined by experience and customer satisfaction ratings.

New Fiverr sellers can offer two gig extras at prices of $5, $10, or $20. The highest Fiverr level, called a Top Rated Seller, can offer six gig extras at prices up to $100 or more. Additionally a New Seller can only offer seven gigs at a time, while a Top Rated Seller can have thirty active gigs.

How It Works

At Fiverr, you are rewarded for being creative and having unique skills. Just browse the site and you'll find all sorts of interesting gigs that range from the mundane to the absolutely bizarre! For instance, if you purchase one gig, a very attractive woman will make you a video of her singing "Happy Birthday" to you for only $10. Or, if you need assistance with a script, an experienced programmer will write an Excel macro and script for just $5. So, the more creative you are with your offering, the more you will stand out and the more you'll sell.

Getting started on Fiverr is easy. To join, click the button at Fiverr's website header, choose a profile name, and confirm your email. From there, click the Become a Seller button and set up your profile, including availability, skills, and descriptions of what you will offer. Then create your first gig!

To keep your feedback rating high, respond professionally and promptly to any query, as you must maintain a four-star rating to move on to the next Fiverr level.

The amount you can make from Fiverr will depend on your Fiverr level and how much time you can put into providing efficient and quality services for your customers. Fiverr does take a 20% commission on any purchase below $20 and 5% above $20. That still leaves you with $4 for a simple $5 gig. So, if you only did one gig a day, you could easily make $120 per month. Because Fiverr allows sellers to offer stepped pricing through Gig Extras, one gig could be $100 (or more). Imagine if you did one $100 gig every day? You'd earn a whopping $2,850—after you pay Fiverr its commission.

How many gigs can you complete per day? The possibilities are endless.

When It Pays

When someone places an order, Fiverr collects the funds and puts them in escrow. Once a project is approved, funds are released into a Fiverr account and sit there for fourteen days (for regular providers) and seven days (for Top Rated providers). After this period has passed, you can then withdraw payment from your Fiverr account.

How It Pays

Fiverr pays contractors via PayPal or the Fiverr Revenue Card, supported by Payoneer. There is a $20 minimum to use the Fiverr Revenue Card.

Advanced tips for succeeding at Fiverr:

- When you create a gig, use concise and powerful descriptions that completely spell out what you are selling.

- Do your best to reach as many people as possible. Keep it powerful, short, and sweet.

- Before you offer your own gig, do some research to see what several of the top gig sellers are offering. Then see if you can offer something comparable or even better.

- Set clear parameters for your gig, like a defined turnaround time. Fiverr clients can cancel late projects and give negative feedback for untimely work.

- Use appropriate tag words so clients can find your gigs.

- After completing a gig, send a brief message to your buyer, asking them to give you a good rating if satisfied with your work. Great ratings will go a long way in attracting future buyers.

Fiverr is an incredible and fun way to make extra money. By working hard to build a solid clientele base, exceeding expectations by delivering quality work, and always doing your best, you can rake in the dough and make your financial dreams come true.

Where to Sign Up: https://www.fiverr.com/

Nonbidding Freelance Site #4 – crowdSPRING

For people who have great web designing, copywriting, branding, or graphic designing skills—but don't want to deal with the headaches of pitching proposals, bidding on projects, and interviewing with prospective clients—crowdSPRING might be the perfect solution for you. Through crowdSPRING, you can connect with hundreds of clients looking for talented professionals to create a clever logo, dynamic website, outstanding copy, and more.

How It Works

Unlike other sites where you compete for their business, clients are competing to give you their money for your creative works. Kind of a nice concept, right? This site is like a reverse marketplace. Keep in mind that buyers receive over ninety-one entries per project. Business owners choose a category, list the price they're willing to pay for the project, how soon they need it completed, and afterward tell the team what they require. Then the ideas come rolling in.

The business owners can ask for revisions, if needed, and, when they see a concept they like (or love), they hire the freelancer to complete the project. The freelancer who is selected is paid, and everyone is happy. And, if you'd rather not work with the crowd, you can work one-on-one with a designer, and you'll still receive a legal contract, project management tools, and great customer service.

For the buyer, the opportunity is 100% risk free since crowdSPRING guarantees that the buyer will be happy with the finished work product. Once payments are rendered, the buyer owns the material.

Let's flip the coin for a second and look at how great crowdSPRING works if you are one of the creative design people, or "creatives," looking to bid on a job. A veritable smorgasbord of potential jobs and contacts awaits you in your field as a creative.

Registration is simple. You give them your name and email address, and, after a confirmation email, you are ready to bid on jobs. On the site, you'll make a bid to complete the projects listed on the dashboard. You can preview the task and submit a bid or pass it over if it doesn't seem like the best fit. You can upload your attempts at meeting the client's request, and prospective clients are allowed to come back to the bidders with any revisions before selecting one winner. Once the task is successfully completed, crowdSPRING pays you through either PayPal or Payoneer.

Over fifty thousand projects have been completed using the site, and it is quickly becoming a popular marketplace for businesses to get the design work they need and for designers to find interesting work. Before committing as a creative on the site, you can browse through some projects, look at creatives' portfolios, and sign up for the newsletter and blog. Joining is free though, so why not get on board with one of the fastest growing communities of designers and employers? This is the next wave of consumer marketing. Gone are the days of fifteen-person teams, churning out ideas late into the night. Here, potential employers can pick from people around the world, each with a unique insight to bring to the project.

How It Pays

If you're a new creative, you won't get paid until thirty days after your first project wraps up.

When It Pays

Once your first project has been paid out, crowdSPRING pays every Monday, Wednesday, and Friday. If you're just getting started, working on projects for the site can be a great way to build your portfolio and potentially earn a little bit of cash in the process.

Here are some advanced tips:

- Brush up on your marketable skills. Don't be afraid to take classes which enhance your writing or design skills. The more training you have, the more likely you are to please your clients.

- Keep it simple. Uncomplicated and meaningful designs that stir emotions within the client are always best.

- Capture a business owner's vision. Listen carefully to the client's vision and try to replicate it. Don't ignore the client's wishes because you think you have a better idea of how things should be done. Instead, create a design that brings their vision to life. Simple is always better than extravagant.

- Showcase your work. Don't be afraid to build your reputation by showcasing your work via social media outlets like Instagram, Facebook, or Twitter.

- Use failure as feedback. If you aren't chosen for a project, don't get discouraged. Art is subjective, and the business owner may have simply liked another style better. Study the chosen designs.

- Treat each client like royalty. Always put forth your best work—no matter what. Communicate openly with clients to ensure you're on the same page. Always do more than you're asked. For instance, if you're working on a small logo-rebranding project, you still must utilize your skills to wow your client. You still must think the project through and create an amazing logo, just like you would for a complete website design project. After all, if you do a great job on the logo, you may be hired for more complicated projects.

Where to Sign Up: https://www.crowdSPRING.com/

8. How To Make Money with Online Chat Jobs

Have you ever visited a website and come across a live help chat button? You know the unobtrusive kind that reads Live Help or the more smack-you-in-your-face popup that says, "Can I help you?" Either way, companies (both big and small) understand that e-commerce is the wave of the future, and these companies are willing to hire online chat operators to assist their clients for a more "personalized shopping experience."

This actually makes sense because e-commerce is huge, growing more and more every day. According to *Internet Retailer*, e-commerce in the United States grew by 14.6% in 2015, accounting for one-third of all retail sales in the country. Online chat options buoyed e-commerce as it aided in propping consumer confidence in transacting online.

Besides that, this type of engagement increases customer loyalty and satisfaction, retention rates, and sales. Companies—like American Express, HostGator, Weight Watchers, Coach—use chat representatives.

But how much money can you make as an online chat representative? Based on the Tempe survey, the average income of an online chat representative as of September 2016 is approximately $23,000 USD. Not bad, working from the comforts of your own home.

The Job Scope

The job of a website chat representative can be done on a full-time or part-time basis. The basic job responsibilities are to:

- Provide customers with more information to make a buying decision

- Empathetically listen and respond to questions or concerns

- Accept orders, confirm charges, ship and track items, etc.
- Help customers with the management of their accounts
- Record online chats for later reference
- Improve sales and marketing efforts
- Refer customers to proper channels

In order to excel at this role, you must be skilled in communicating (written and verbal). You'll also need basic computer skills and must have at least a high school diploma. Most companies will provide the training, but you might have to supply the equipment, which consists of a computer (desktop or laptop) with a camera, headset, and microphone. For the first three months or so, companies may closely evaluate chat reps at their home office, but, after this training period, most companies will allow you to work from home.

For those able to handle the work schedule, the wide variety of customers, and the demand for patience, the financial rewards can be worth the effort. The growth projection for this job is about 13% across the board. The competition, if it can be considered that, would be automated technology or artificial intelligence.

Companies You Can Apply To

Does this sound like an opportunity you'd want to pursue? Some of the top companies—always on the lookout for online chat representatives—are:

Chat Job Opportunity #1 – Apple at Home

As a home-based job with Apple, the base pay is $15 an hour. Apple is accepting applicants from all states and even offers profit sharing, cash bonuses, and stock bonuses. You'll also get an Apple Mac, which you can take home to use, but you must supply your own Internet and assign a dedicated landline for work.

You must commit to a schedule and be ready to work on weekends. If you pass the Skype interview, you will be asked to attend a six-week training course and must agree to working hours from 7:00 a.m. to

10:30 p.m., on a shifting basis.

Where to Apply: https://www.apple.com/jobs/us/aha.html

Chat Job Opportunity #2 – LivePerson

The average take-home income of a LivePerson rep is $63,000. LivePerson is a solutions company with main offices based in New York, so working with them means being assigned to any of their clients.

You will appear on the company's roster as an expert, detailing your skills, knowledge, and experience. As an expert, you have access to all LivePerson tools, and you will be allowed to network with other experts and in-house employees.

Where to Apply: http://www.liveperson.com/company/careers

Chat Job Opportunity #3 – Arise

Arise hires independent contractors to work as their chat agents. These representatives work from home for an hourly wage of $9 to $14. However, the business arrangement is between you and the Arise client, not directly with Arise. This means you get your clients using the Arise portal, and the client will pay you. Payouts are done twice a month through bank deposits.

With this company, you are allowed to select the client program you want to work with and your schedule. Arise considers you as a business partner, so you are required to put up a small capital investment of at least $250. This amount should cover your start-up costs in setting up your home business, like securing the business permit, applying for a landline phone with a keypad and headset, and taking their certification course. You must also provide your own computer and Internet service.

If you would rather not set up a new business, your other option would be to tie-in with an existing business linked with Arise and become a part of their virtual solution.

Where to Apply: http://www.arise.com/

Chat Job Opportunity #4 – Needle

Needle was established in 2009 and counts companies like Under Armour, Skullcandy, and Norton among its top clients. If you decide to work with Needle, you will serve as a chat support agent, working from home, selling the client's products online.

The going rate of pay is about $10 an hour, but you can earn incentive points to boost this income with your performance and the feedback from clients. Points are not convertible to cash but can be exchanged for client products.

Payout is done every Monday using PayPal. If you agree to work with Needle, you must commit to a flexible schedule arranged at least six hours before you have to work. To get the schedule you want, you must compete with the other freelancers or work as a free skate, which means working on leftover schedules (or schedules that no one wanted).

To get started with Needle, you must pass their interview done via chat. If you are accepted, you will get a welcome email. They also have an online application process, but these are usually reserved for specific positions within the company.

Where to Apply: https://register.needle.com/

Chat Job Opportunity #5 – Uber

Ridesharing and chauffeur-servicing Uber is not just looking for drivers with cars. Money can be made as one of their off-site support reps. However, this is a full-time job of basically sending and receiving emails that pays $10 to $15 an hour.

You must work forty hours a week, which means a weekly take-home pay of $400 minimum. Once you are hired, you must attend a three-day training course, and, upon completion, you are given a set schedule and will be asked to sign a nondisclosure agreement.

As an employee, you get Uber discounts, insurance, vacation leaves, and 401k plans. You must provide your own computer and high-speed Internet.

The negative feedback about Uber is the amount of stress and demand on your time because the company is growing quickly at a speed-of-light pace.

Where to Apply: https://www.uber.com/careers/

9. Make Money with Micro Job Sites

A micro job is usually a temporary task-type job. These jobs are often done on the Internet, and the work may include being a virtual assistant, writing blog posts, conducting research, executing simple data entry, or other errands. The income made from these types of jobs varies from website to website. Doing micro jobs allows people to earn extra money from the comfort of their homes. Micro job sites are growing rapidly and are in great demand.

Micro Job Site #1 – Amazon Mechanical Turk or MTurk

One popular micro jobs website is Amazon Mechanical Turk or MTurk. This website is a crowdsourcing program where you earn money by performing basic tasks or HITs (human intelligence tasks). Most of the HITs are simple to do, such as completing surveys, copying text from photos and scans, rewriting sentences, completing surveys, entering data from a receipt into a form, writing articles, and transcribing audio files.

How It Works

Becoming a Mechanical Turk worker is easy, especially if you already have an Amazon account. You simply sign up and start working on HITs.

Most of the lower-paying HITs are available to anyone. As the HITs increase in value, certain certifications are required—either through the Amazon platform or through a third-party qualification test (e.g., through MTurk Requesters Speechpad and TryMyUI). Obtaining the certifications is generally worth it, as you can make more money in a shorter period of time.

Here are some tips to finding good HITs on MTurk:

- Use the search option to find the type of HITs you want to work on.

- Avoid the $0.01 HITs.

- Be sure to understand what the HIT is for before accepting it.

- Browse the daily Awesome HITs thread on the forum.

Another useful website is MTurk List. The website list is always being updated with MTurk HITs, and the site is powered by MTurk users. The users can provide details about each HIT, such as pay, the star rating, and the requester's name and rating. The HITs can also be marked as dead if no longer available at that time.

The Greasy Fork is an MTurk page-monitoring website that has many scripts for MTurk users. Some of them can be used for snagging HITs, reviewing requesters, keeping track of the HITs you've done, and much more.

Once you find a HIT, you work on it, and the requester approves it. Your funds are then transferred to your dashboard and earnings page. If you live in the United States or India, you can transfer your funds on your earnings page to your bank account, or you can receive Amazon gift cards. The choice is yours. If you're in other countries, you can only get Amazon gift cards as payments. **Note:** New users must wait ten days before receiving payments or gift cards.

What It Pays

HIT values range from $0.01 to over $100, depending on the time and skill required.

When It Pays

It pays when you request a funds transfer from your earnings page.

Advanced Tips to Succeed at MTurk:

1. Below you will find information on how to protect yourself from identity theft and scams. Remember, if it sounds too good to be true, it probably is.

2. You will want to stay away from HITs that ask you for personal information, such as your email address, full name, physical address, or credit card information. A genuine HIT will not ask for any personal information from you.

3. Another way to protect yourself from bad requesters on HITs is to install the Turkopticon toolbar. The toolbar allows you to point at any of the requesters' names on the site, and a drop-down box will show you what other workers say about that requester. You may want to avoid those requesters who have a bad rating, just to be sure that you will get paid for the work that you do.

4. Another way to stay on top of things happening in the MTurk world is to follow forums. The two main forums are Turker Nation and MTurk Forum. Here you will have access to the views of other MTurk workers, allows you to be on the lookout for poor requesters and jobs, and a good place to see what kind of positive experiences others are having.

Where to Sign Up: https://www.mturk.com/mturk/welcome

Micro Job Site #2 – Microworkers

Microworkers is a website where you can make money doing small jobs. The jobs are simple, quick (only taking a few minutes to complete), and are often referred to as micro jobs. Some types of jobs you may see on Microworkers range from conducting online research, visiting websites to perform usability tests, posting blog or forum comments, signing up for referral programs, downloading and testing applications, creating backlinks, or participating in forums.

How It Works

Join Microworkers for free. This site also welcomes international users. As a contractor, you are not employed by the website, and you can set your own hours. The amount of money you make is entirely up to you. Work a lot, make a lot.

To find micro jobs, click on the Tasks link and browse through the listed tasks. Each of the tasks will have information on how long it will take to complete, what you will be paid, and any special instructions.

Once you find a micro job you wish to complete, accept this job and start working on it. Be careful to follow all the instructions, or the task will not be accepted, and you won't be paid.

When you complete projects, you receive a success rating. This rating system encourages freelancers to do their best, as a negative rating will bring down your success rating and prevent you from obtaining future tasks. To ensure that you keep your success rating high, take jobs that you know you can complete and do them in a timely manner.

The more successful tasks you finish, the more stars you will receive in certain categories. The stars reflect your reputation, which employers evaluate when they're searching for people to add to their list of favorites or Hire Group. The higher your reputation in a category, the better your chances of getting hired within a Hire Group.

If you are asked to revise a task, click the Revise button and update the task when you have made the necessary changes. This ensures that your rating stays high and that you get paid for your efforts.

The amount of available tasks will depend on what time zone the client is in. Therefore, it makes sense to check the site at random times, day and night, to improve your chances of receiving quality tasks.

What It Pays

The amount you earn will depend on the projects you accept.

When It Pays

You must earn at least $9 plus fees before placing a request to withdraw your money from Microworkers. Once you have reached this amount, click on the Withdrawal link to send your money to you via PayPal, Skrill, or bank transfer. **Note:** Bank transfers typically take three to five business days. Also your first withdrawal will require a PIN to be activated. This PIN will be mailed to you. PIN delivery can take up to one to four weeks, so keep this in mind when requesting your first payout.

Payments are made twice a week on Wednesdays and Sundays.

Where to Sign Up: https://microworkers.com/

Micro Job Site #3 – Clickworker

Clickworker is a Germany-based company that states it is a "cloud-based service, based on human intelligence that gets work done." Basically, in plain English, they're another established micro job site that pays you to complete tasks (HITs) from your desired location. Like other micro job sites, you are in control of how much you work and how much money you make. The more you work, the more you earn.

Typically individuals can earn between $5–$30 per hour on Clickworker. The rates you'll receive will depend on many factors, including your experience with particular HITs, the speed at which you work, the complexity of the tasks, and so on.

How It Works

Residents of the United States can sign up to be a Clickworker. However, if you are a US citizen, you will must provide a valid social security number to get paid. If you do not live in the States, you will need a bank account in a SEPA (Single Euro Payments Area) country or a valid PayPal account.

PayPal users are paid once a week between Wednesday and Friday. If your money is to be deposited into your bank account, you are only paid once a month.

To get started, set up an account on Clickworker and then include all requested information, including your PayPal information. Next, go to Assessments and get qualified. As you will only have access to tasks that you are qualified to do, you must get prequalified.

Each qualification requires the passing of a short exam. Do your best on each exam, as some of the assessment tests may not be retaken if you don't pass the first time. Some qualification exams, like the Placement Test exam, contain easy multiple-choice questions about basic grammar; whereas others, like UHRS (Universal Human Relevance System) qualifications, are more complicated and may evaluate a combination of research and language questions.

The amount of time to complete a HIT will vary from task to task. A countdown timer displays on your work page when you begin a task. This way, you stay on track to complete the task on time. If you run out of time while doing a task, the task will be canceled and taken from you.

You may also notice that, at times, lots of tasks are available, and, at others, there aren't any. The work ebbs and flows. Sometimes it is because the projects have all been completed, and, at other times, it is because you don't meet specific requirements for the group. For instance, if they need native speakers or someone who has special knowledge, and you don't meet those requirements, you won't be eligible. One cool feature is that you can hide tasks that you are not interested in and unhide these tasks at any time.

The money you make from doing a task will not show up in your account until the requester has approved your work. Your work can be approved in a few hours or a few days. Sometimes it could take weeks for the money to show in your account. This does not happen often.

When It Pays

UHRS projects are paid twenty-one days after completion, and other projects are paid seven days after processing.

How It Pays

Clickworker pays via PayPal or your bank account.

Additional tips:

1. Get qualified for as many opportunities as you can! The more qualified you are, the more opportunities you'll see, and the more money you can potentially make.

2. Follow all guidelines. Read them once, read them twice, and read them again for good measure. If previous HITs are available, do them before moving forward with the qualification exam!

3. Take your time when completing qualifications, as you only get a certain amount of attempts. To improve your chances of passing, think carefully about the answers.

4. Don't rush when you're completing tasks. Work carefully at all times and double-check your work. Don't just click for the sake of clicking. You will get caught.

5. Check your accuracy under My Reports, showing how many tasks you got right (1.0 is perfect and decreases with every incorrect answer). A score of .75 might get you booted out, so be careful. **Note:** If you consistently get HITs wrong, don't sweat it. Just move on to another set and don't take it personally. It happens and is no indication of how incredible you are!

Where to Sign Up: http://www.clickworker.com/

Micro Job Site #4 – Lionbridge VirtualBee/The Smart Crowd

Lionbridge hosts a crowdsourcing platform called Lionbridge Smart Crowd, meant for home-based jobs. The work is flexible and part-time, and, according to their website, related to IT and non-IT projects and business processes. Rates are dependent upon the type of task and the location of the worker or VirtualBee.

How It Works

After registering to be a part of The Smart Crowd, Lionbridge will have you take an online assessment. After passing the assessment test, you can work on tasks and assignments. If your country isn't located on the career page of current opportunities, Lionbridge states that you can still contact them through the website form for consideration. Those who pass the assessments are considered contract employees and thus can create their own schedules.

The jobs vary daily but include data entry (numbers only or letters only), English language data research, and multilanguage data research—including Chinese, French, German, Italian, Japanese, Spanish, Polish, Korean, Russian, and Portuguese.

Generally the foreign languages data research pays more per keystroke but also requires a proficiency in the listed language and English. The Smart Crowd is a great place to get data entry experience if a newcomer to the field.

What It Pays

Generally the pay rate varies from roughly $0.20 per one thousand keystrokes up to $0.60 per one thousand keystrokes, and it is not recommended to be a sole source of income but rather something to make some extra cash and/or gain data entry experience.

When It Pays

They pay contractors monthly via Dwolla, a pay site similar to PayPal. You can get a Dwolla debit card or you can transfer the funds to a personal checking/savings account online.

Additional Strategies to Help You Succeed:

- The quicker you are at typing, the more you can complete in a shorter span of time.

- Check back frequently, as the jobs up for grabs change frequently. Occasionally nothing is posted when checking one hour, but checking back the following hour may yield postings.

- The schedules are flexible, allowing you to work when you want, but it is recommended, as with all contractor jobs, that you set a time in the day dedicated to completing the listed jobs.

Where to Sign Up: https://thesmartcrowd.lionbridge.com/

Micro Job Site #5 – Spare5

Spare5 is a crowdsourcing website that allows individuals (around the globe) to complete tasks in their free time. Many of the tasks can be done in as little as five minutes and are a lot of fun. Tasks might include creating keywords, finding celebrity Twitter handles or lawyers' addresses, finding objects in images, matching products, etc.

The tasks change regularly so it's best to check on a daily basis.

The pay runs from $0.01–$0.50 per task.

How It Works

To get started, sign up at Spare5 using Facebook, Google, LinkedIn, or an email address. They not only have a web-based system where you can retrieve tasks but also an on-the-go iPhone app. They don't have an app for Android users yet, but they're working on it. The tasks on the app are different from those available on the website, so you could essentially use both methods to make more money.

Once you sign up with Spare5, you can browse through the list of available tasks. As stated previously, the tasks vary and may require qualification before you can choose them. Once you pass the short qualification exam, you can get to work. The good thing about passing qualification tests is that you'll then have access to tasks that pay a bit higher.

Usually you'll find many tasks to keep you busy. However, sometimes no tasks are available to work on. Therefore, it makes sense to visit the site at random times to increase your odds of finding tasks.

When you have selected the task you want to work on, take your time to read the instructions carefully. If you complete tasks, and your work is high-quality, then you will gain access to more tasks. If your work isn't high-quality, you will lose access to tasks in the future. One way to keep your tasks rated highly is to read the instructions and watch for any special requests for the task.

How It Pays

The only payout option at this time is PayPal. Your PayPal account must be verified in order for them to send your money. The pay is sent every Friday, and you are paid for tasks that have passed through a quality review and have been accepted by the requester from the Wednesday of the week before. The minimum payout is $1. Anything less than $1 will carry over to the next pay period or until you have earned more than $1.

When It Pays

Spare5 pays for approved tasks during the previous seven-day time period (Wednesday to Wednesday). However, you need at least $1 in your account or the funds roll over until you have accumulated that amount. To see your held amount, you can check the Spare5 app or the Webtask site.

Where to Sign Up: https://spare5.com/

10. Make Money as a Customer Support Specialist

Do you have a gift for gab? Do you like talking to customers and helping to solve problems? If so, working as a customer support specialist might be perfect for you, whereby you might do the following: provide customers with product and service information, listen to complaints and offer solutions, answer questions or make product suggestions, answer phones, evaluate billing accounts and make adjustments, and much more.

To succeed as a customer support specialist, you must have a high school diploma. However, some companies may prefer that you have some college experience. The medial income for this position is $16,640–$31,220 annually or $8–$15 per hour.

Skills Required:

- Pleasant voice plus well-developed verbal and written communication skills
- Able to respond to customer complaints in a timely manner
- Good organizational skills
- General knowledge of Microsoft Office
- Multitasker
- Able to handle irate customers in a calm and professional manner
- Able to take a multitude of calls without getting burned out

Some customer support specialist positions are on-site, but some companies hire virtual workers to work at home. Here's the equipment you'll need:

- Reliable laptop or desktop computer
- Quality headset
- Desk and ergonomic chair
- High-speed Internet access
- Dedicated landline
- Quiet work space

Here are some companies that hire customer support specialists to work from home:

Customer Support Opportunity #1 – 1-800-Flowers

This company is headquartered in Long Island, NY, and is a family-run business, headed by Founder and CEO Jim McCann and President Chris McCann. The company is an online florist that hires remote customer support specialists to work at home.

Customer support specialists will take inbound calls and complete transactions using multiple software applications. Most positions are seasonal or temporary but can lead to being hired as a full-time employee.

Pay starts at around $9 per hour and is paid both on and off the phone. They also offer paid training and benefits to its full-time employees.

Where to Sign Up:

https://www.1800flowers.com/about-us-employment-opportunities/

Customer Support Opportunity #2 – Acanac

Acanac was established in 2004. The company is one of the leading independent providers in telecommunications services. They have expanded their customer service department to offer 24/7 assistance.

Requirements:

- Computer or laptop
- High-speed Internet service
- General computer knowledge
- Quiet work environment
- Fluent in English or French

Pay starts at $10 per hour, and you will be offered a minimum of forty hours per week. You are required to work weekends. They also offer paid training. You can send your résumé to jobs@acanac.com.

Where to Sign Up: https://www.acanac.com/

Customer Support Opportunity #3 – LiveOps

LiveOps was started over fifteen years ago and is innovated by technology that eases the way customer service is initiated. LiveOps has over twenty thousand independent customer support specialists, and they handle over one hundred million calls and more than four hundred clients each year.

As a customer support specialist, you will handle a wide variety of companies, calls, and programs. Once you are a customer support specialist, you can choose additional opportunities that appeal to you.

Phone and computer requirements:

- Corded landline phone; call waiting and voice mail must be disabled
- Corded headset
- Windows-based computer
- High-speed Internet
- Computer virus program

After you apply for the position, you must submit to a background and credit check. This is done by a third-party company and costs $65. This fee is nonrefundable. It can take a couple weeks for the background check and the credit check to be completed.

There are no minimum log-in requirements; however, inactivity can affect your performance statistics. This may cause you to lose your contract with the company. You set your own schedule by blocking thirty minutes at a time. The amount of money you make is dependent on which company you are working for. Some companies pay $0.25 per minute of talk time, while others pay a base rate in addition to bonuses. You are responsible for submitting your invoices to be paid. You will then be paid either by check or direct deposit twice per month.

Where to Sign Up: http://www.liveops.com/company/careers-jobs/

Customer Support Opportunity #4 – Enterprise

Enterprise is a family-owned global network that spans across seventy countries. They have become the leader in the transportation service industry and own more than 1.7 million vehicles.

The Contact Center for Enterprise hires work-from-home customer support specialists to provide exceptional service to their customers. The specialists will answer general and brand questions, communicate policies, handle roadside assistance calls, and research reservations.

Once you have applied for a position, you must complete five weeks of paid training, which takes place between 9:00 a.m. to 5:30 p.m. CST, Monday through Friday. The starting pay for this position is $12.50 per hour with bonuses. Your schedule will be based on the needs of the company and could require you to work mornings, afternoons, and evenings. You will also be required to work weekends.

Requirements:

- Must be able to work in the United States
- Must be at least eighteen years old

- Minimum of one year customer service experience

- Basic computer skills

- Must be available forty hours per week

- Work space must have a smoke detector, a first aid kit, and a fire extinguisher

- High-speed Internet access

Where to Sign Up: https://careers.enterprise.com/category/work-from-home-jobs/430-1626-1625-5496/17267/1

Customer Support Opportunity #5 – NexRep

NexRep is a virtual call center with more than fifty years' experience in call center management. You will be considered an independent contractor, not an employee. You will receive personalized support through NexRep's professional staff so that you may reach your full potential. You will have the freedom to choose when you are available to work. The pay is estimated to be between $15 and $25 per hour, depending on experience. You raise the amount you make by applying various skills, certifications, and experiences.

Requirements:

- Must be legal to work in the United States

- Must reside in the United States

- A quiet work area

- Cell phone or landline

- Must pass a national criminal background check (fee is $25)

Equipment:

- Computer or laptop
- Microsoft Word and Excel
- Windows Vista or newer, or Mac OS X Lion or newer
- Printer
- Noise-canceling USB headset
- High-speed Internet; must be hard-wired to a computer

Where to Sign Up: http://www.nexrep.com/opportunities.html

11. How to Make Money Podcasting

Podcasting is the brand-new talk show. With a podcast, individuals can post digital media files, using their computer or any portable media player, sharing their "message" with others. Last September, CBS MoneyWatch stated that the podcast is now "attracting real money."

For instance, John Lee Dumas, a podcaster from Puerto Rico and founder of EOFire, earned more than $50,000 USD simply by selling spots on his podcast. He also earns around $300,000 from online courses. How did he get to this point? Dumas was in real estate and listened to podcasts while on the road. He decided to start his own podcast and launched EOFire, or Entrepreneurs on Fire, in 2012. He does daily podcasts and features successful entrepreneurs only.

His June 2016 gross earnings reached over $214,000 with only $65,223 as his total expenses, which means he made over $149,000 in the month of June alone! More exciting for you to know is that he stresses it only takes an investment of $500 and a laptop to get started as a podcaster. This makes it an economical opportunity for individuals with excellent communication skills.

With more and more people connecting online, this moneymaking opportunity isn't going anywhere. Statistics show that, from 2015 to 2016, podcast listening grew as much as 23%. Hundreds of people, like Dumas mentioned above, are making great incomes via podcasting, and millions of others are enjoying the talents of great podcasters.

To get started, record your podcast. You can do this in two ways. You can record straight from your computer, or use devices such as a digital recorder and mixer. The digital recorder is recommended over recording right to your computer. This is because computers can have technical issues and corrupt files, and a digital recorder places the data directly onto a SD card. Using a dynamic microphone is much better because it will not pick up so much of the surrounding noises while you record. They are perfect for recording in a small room. If you are using a digital recorder, you do not need to purchase a mixer.

You can also download an app to your iOS or Android device so that you may record your podcast on the go. Some of them are:

- Opinion Podcasts – This iPod touch, iPad, and iPhone app allows users to easily edit, record, and publish podcasts; and then share them via iTunes Podcast Directory, Facebook, Twitter, Google Drive, Dropbox, and more. Both the free and paid versions require iOs 7.1 or later.

- Bossjock Studio – This app is available for iPhone, iPad, and iPod touch. It enables users to podcast on the go. Features include voiceover capability, ability to encode to popular formats (MP3, WAV, AIFF), edit and fine-tune playback, receive live audio, and more. This app costs $9.99 and requires iOs 7.1 or later.

- Speaker Studio – This easy-to-operate Android app enables users to turn their phone into a fully functioning radio studio, where you can prerecord podcasts or broadcast live. You can even mix channels, add sound effects, and add personalized tracks. You can share on Twitter and Facebook, and interact with listeners via live chat.

To start making money with your podcast, find a profitable niche. Here are some ways to find yours:

- Love what you are talking about.

- Pinpoint what topic interests you the most.

- Decide what topic will provide you enough content to fill your podcast for a long time.

Finding a sponsor is a great way to make money with your podcast. Sponsors are not only interested in the amount of people you have subscribed to your podcast but they are also looking at how engaged your audience is. Things to have in place before you approach a sponsor should be:

- A great podcast with great content, production, and presentation

- Know your audience numbers

- Know your audience: how engaged are they?

You can also use affiliate programs to generate money through your podcast. You can promote your affiliate link through your podcast to generate money as your listeners click the link. The affiliate income will build over time. The more content you provide, the better your reputation. You can also offer promo codes to your listeners as an incentive for them to click on your affiliate link.

Some affiliate programs you may want to use are:

- Blubrry – This company allows you to earn rewards for promoting and selling services offered at blubrry.com.

- Amazon – Free to join. You choose what products you advertise to your audience.

- Clickbank – This is a good program for beginners in the affiliate market. They offer great service and educational support to their users.

Through your podcast, you can also offer to your audience your coaching and consulting services on a one-on-one basis. You are basically offering your expertise as a service and charging members of your audience for your one-on-one attention.

Generating income through your podcast will take time to build. You have the potential to make hundreds to thousands of dollars a month with the right niche. However, you must build traffic first. This can be done via various online and off-line marketing methods, including social media marketing, blogging, strategic partnerships with other well-known podcasters, and more.

Here are a few tricks of the trade to help you get ahead of the others and make some serious moola.

1. Offer real value. Your podcasts should give value to your listeners and not just be about a person giving his views and opinions. This style cannot sustain an audience unless you already have celebrity status and a loyal following.

2. Observe proper ethics. When you have guests, let them speak. When you talk, speak professionally, avoid cuss words or anything that could be misconstrued as offensive. If you must voice a harsh opinion, give your listeners a heads-up by saying this is your personal view, and you have no intentions of making anyone feel uncomfortable.

3. Be inspiring and authentic. Avoid thinking about the potential earnings because you might come across as a hard-sell and concerned more about what you can gain rather than what your listeners can learn from your podcast.

4. Be prepared to work hard and smart. This means understanding that it isn't all about content but also about marketing. The money is in advertising and finding sponsors. You can survive beautifully on just one sponsor if you truly believe in the product and are willing to stake your reputation.

5. Follow trends. By trends, this refers to the feedback from your listeners. They will provide you with leads on the direction to take your podcast through their comments. So allow comments to be posted publicly because this, in itself, is a powerful marketing angle you'd be crazy to skip.

12. Making Money Answering Questions Online

In the good old days, people had libraries in their homes, and most families had a full set of encyclopedias as well. People weren't afraid to spend money on education, and they really relied on their encyclopedias to find the information they needed. Since then, online encyclopedias are popular, but now most people use search engines to find the information they need. Oftentimes, however, they can't find what they need and turn to experts to give them answers quickly. These experts are knowledgeable about their assigned subject matter and can quickly answer questions from users with a combination of knowledge, research skills, and professional experience.

If you are an expert, skilled in certain areas, an outstanding researcher, or an educated worker who wants to share your knowledge with others, you can earn extra income by answering questions responsibly. Here are some of these websites hiring experts like you:

Q&A Company #1 – ChaCha.com

ChaCha.com is a search engine powered by humans. It was launched in 2006 as an app and offers two positions: Expeditor Guides and General Specialist Guides. The Expeditors get paid $0.02 for every session while the Specialists get paid $0.10–$0.20 per session, all via PayPal. This means you can make around $100 for answering twenty thousand questions.

Right now ChaCha is not accepting new applicants, but they are accepting your contact details for future openings.

Where to Sign Up: http://www.chacha.com/

Q&A Company #2 – LivePerson.com

As a LivePerson, you get assigned to a client who can come from anywhere around the world. When you sign up (for free), you are screened and placed under the Expert category. All the tools are at your disposal for free. You will receive messages from the client and will answer the questions posted through the messaging system.

This app was launched in 1995 and has been doing very well with over $209 million in revenues. They charge their clients a monthly rate based on the number of people assigned to their account. Thus, if you work for them, you get assigned to a specific client as part of a team. They mostly have salaried employees and are known for having a great office culture.

Where to Sign Up: http://www.liveperson.com/company/careers

Q&A Company #3 – Experts123.com

This website is used mostly by American males and is around nine years old. It has an excellent reputation as a community of experts and passionate people. They accept specialists from around the world who can expertly give their recommendations in an easy-to-use Q&A service. You must register with them and provide reasons why you are an expert. You must also be adept at writing intelligently.

Most of those who sign up with this website are freelance writers who want to continue working on flextime. It has an income-sharing setup and an upfront payment scheme. The income-sharing is $2 for each one thousand views of accepted work. Upfront pay is only given after you have established your reputation as an expert and can pay as much as $20/article.

Payouts are done through PayPal with a minimum amount of $20.

Where to Sign Up: https://www.experts123.com/

Q&A Company #4 – JustAnswer.com

Launched in 2003, JustAnswer is a question-answer community forum with verified experts in different fields. They have a customer base of twenty million, and a reputation for being responsive and responsible in making sure that customers are satisfied with the answers.

To become a member of their expert community, apply online and completely fill out the profile form. Then take a short test to verify your skills and knowledge. Finally you must submit proof of credentials, like a diploma, certifications, and work experience, and agree to a background check.

Experts get paid a portion of the money deposited by the person inquiring if the question was answered satisfactorily. Payouts are done through PayPal, credit and debit cards, and also prepaid gift cards.

As you can see, many options exist if you want to make money answering questions, whether it be on a freelance basis or as an employee.

Where to Sign Up: http://www.justanswer.com/

13. Make Money with Social Media Marketing

Social media marketing is simply using social media to get people to like your product, service, business, or endeavor. Although it sounds easy enough, it is actually quite complex and a bit difficult to master. It can potentially build up (or break down) a business because it deals with perception and the social aspect of marketing.

According to Statista, social media marketing is all about engagement and is why Facebook continues to be the leading platform for most businesses. However, when it comes down to interaction, Instagram is the clear dominant player across 130 industries and forty thousand companies, with fifty-one million posts.

Today, 84% of business-to-business entrepreneurs use social media for several reasons:

- It drives targeted traffic.
- It boosts search engine optimization (SEO) efforts.
- It helps build strategic relationships.
- It's social and thus friendlier.
- It's cost-effective and can boost the email marketing campaign of all types of businesses.
- It allows entrepreneurs to respond quickly to consumers.
- It builds brand loyalty.
- It introduces products and services to a wider market.

How popular is social media? It is now the #1 activity on the Internet. Interestingly companies can increase their revenues by 40% using social media. Plus, when businesses combine it with other marketing methods, their profits explode.

So, if you're interested in getting your piece of the social media pie, the good news is that now you can. Companies are actually pairing with social media advertising companies to find marketers who can spread the word through their social networks and are willing to pay them for their efforts.

To be a social media marketer, aside from having active social media accounts with all the top social media platforms, you need skills, preferably advanced, in the following:

1. Goal setting and planning
2. Knowledge of how to build a brand and an online reputation
3. Management of content
4. SEO and how to generate inbound traffic
5. Knowledge regarding cultivation of leads and sales
6. Innate creativeness and knowledge of visual effects and design
7. Clear understanding of social advertising and engagement strategies
8. Ability to analyze and measure return on investment (ROI)

If you have a large and active network, at least a few thousand active followers, or are willing to get one, you can certainly make money as a social media marketer. Social media marketers who have at least fifty thousand can charge as high as $50 or as low as $1 for every tweet or post. The range is so wide because it depends on the market you want to reach.

For instance, a social media marketer for a celebrity will be competing with hundreds of other marketers, so demand is not as high for his services as for a social media marketer who specializes in everything to do with space and the universe. Thus, clients look for value over price and subscriber base, because the bottom line is getting a return on their investment.

To give you an idea of how much a single tweet can make, a social media marketer with a Twitter account and three million followers can charge up to $2,000 for his services!

Some of the ways to use social media to make money and create side income are through these sites:

Social Media Marketing Advertising Company #1 – PaidPerTweet

PaidPerTweet is a website that allows users with Twitter accounts to generate some side income. The website allows users to set a price for sharing websites, promotions, etc. The sign-up process is easy and free. This website is a great way to monetize your social media accounts. Companies can hire you to promote messages on your Twitter account.

In order to get started, you need a decent number of followers. You also must create an updated profile, set your prices, and get your Twitter account verified. There are no set rates, but people charge up to $200 for tweeting. However, for a newcomer, it's a good idea to start your bid lower, around $30–$50.

Where to Sign Up: http://www.paidpertweet.com

Social Media Marketing Advertising Company #2 – SponsoredTweets

SponsoredTweets is another website that allows users to charge a price-per-click for ads they tweet. Users are allowed to select from a list of ads updated on a regular basis. To be an eligible user, one must have at least fifty followers, one hundred tweets, and a Twitter account more than sixty days old. This website also allows companies and brands to tap into the followers of Twitter users, and, in return, those users get paid to distribute the company's message.

Cash withdrawals can be made once $50 has accumulated and, for Pro accounts, once $25 has accumulated.

Where to Sign Up: http://www.sponsoredtweets.com

Social Media Marketing Advertising Company #3 – loop88

The loop88 site connects brands with users on Pinterest who can help these brands with their campaigns. In order to get started, sign up with loop88 using your Pinterest username. Specify what categories you usually pin in, e.g., clothes, home decor, etc. Brands are now free to find you and send you an offer to work with them.

Once the work is completed, the money is paid within one day. The total one can make is dependent on charges per pin which can start from $5. The loop88 website usually recommends a rate based on the number of your Pinterest followers.

Where to Sign Up: http://www.loop88.com

14. Make Money with Transcription

Are you a fast typist? Have you ever transcribed documents? Do you enjoy transcribing? Working at home as a transcriptionist gives you the flexibility to set your own hours and work as much or as little as you wish. Most transcription jobs are broken down into general, medical, or legal categories. If you are just starting out in the transcription field, you may want to look for job opportunities in the general category. The medical and legal categories sometimes (but not always) require that you have some degree of education or experience.

Companies that hire transcriptionists may require that you have a foot pedal and a transcribing software package on your computer. Your speed and skill level will affect how much you are paid to do transcription.

Here is a list of companies that hire people to work at home as a transcriptionist:

Transcription Company #1 – TranscribeMe

TranscribeMe was founded in New Zealand in 2011 and is headquartered in the San Francisco Bay Area. They hire transcribers from all over the world. They do require that those applying for a position with their company have a strong understanding of the English language and that they have a decent typing speed. You are not required to have any special equipment other than a computer with Google Chrome and a reliable Internet connection.

To get started, register an account and take their Transcriber Training program. If you can successfully complete the training course, you will be notified when your account is activated. You are not required to work any minimum or maximum number of hours.

What It Pays

TranscribeMe pays $20 per audio hour for general transcription. Other projects will have a higher rate of pay. However, you also have opportunities to move up the ladder and become a Quality Assurance agent, who edits, proofreads, and consolidates transcriptions.

When It Pays

You can request payment weekly, and it will be sent to your PayPal account.

Where to Sign Up: http://transcribeme.com/

Transcription Company #2 – Quicktate/iDictate

Quicktate and iDictate were founded in 2008 and are based in San Francisco, California. Quicktate LLC is a subsidiary of iDictate Inc. Quicktate transcribes memos, voice-mail messages, legal files, medical files, letters, conference calls, recordings of phone calls, and other audio recordings. Some of the audio files could be two to three minutes long, and some could be several hours long. The iDictate transcribers also transcribe all types of files, except voice-mail messages.

This is what the company requires:

- Accurate punctuation and spelling
- Ability to follow instructions
- Typists who can listen to audio files and accurately type what was heard
- Honesty, reliability, and integrity
- Experienced and professional transcriptionists
- An office and/or work space
- No prior felonies or misdemeanors on one's record
- Taking a typing quiz for each specialty that interests you
- Taking a test to prove you understand Quicktate's requirements

Active Income Streams

What It Pays

You can select your own hours and days that you work. The pay for Quicktate is $0.01 per four words typed, and iDictate pays $0.02 per four words typed. You will be paid weekly through PayPal.

Where to Sign Up:

iDictate - http://idictate.com/

Quicktate - http://www.quicktate.com/

Transcription Company #3 – SpeakWrite

SpeakWrite was founded in 1997, and the company helps other companies, organizations, institutions, and individuals increase productivity. Independent contractors have the flexibility to work at home and set their own hours. You will need a background check because of the sensitive nature of the work.

Requirements for Becoming a Transcriptionist:

- You must type at least sixty words per minute with 90% accuracy.

- You must be a legal resident of the United States or Canada.

- You must be proficient in Microsoft Word 2007/2010.

- You must have excellent listening skills.

- You must be able to work independently.

- For legal applicants, you must also have:
    - Two or more years of legal work experience, including transcribing and word processing
    - Experience and knowledge of legal pleadings, court headings, interrogatories, agreements, deposition summaries, etc.

- o Knowledge of proper formatting of legal citations
- For general applicants, you need:
  - o One or more years of word processing and transcribing experience over the last five years
  - o Knowledge and experience of the creation of formal correspondence, memos, reports, etc.

Technology Requirements:

- Windows-based PC
- Windows 7 or higher
- Microsoft Word 2007 or newer
- Internet Explorer v8.0 or higher
- Adobe Acrobat Reader v8.0 or higher
- Windows Media Player v10 or higher
- Sound card
- Earphones
- Printer
- Foot pedal

What It Pays

Once you are accepted as a transcriptionist, you will be paid $0.005 per word transcribed.

When It Pays

You can be paid with check or direct deposit twice a month. Canadian workers are paid by check only.

Where to Sign Up: http://speakwrite.com/

Active Income Streams

Transcription Company #4 – Scribie

Scribie was founded in 2008 by Rajiv Poddar. The company offers transcription services for phone calls, podcasts, interviews, webinars, videos, dictation, and so on. As a transcriber for Scribie, you will listen to audio files and type what you hear as accurately as possible. You must go through a testing process and become certified as a transcriber.

Requirements:

- Comprehension of English
- Verified PayPal account
- Laptop or desktop with Internet connection
- Headphones
- Latest version of Safari, Chrome, or Firefox
- Latest version of Adobe Flash Plug-in

What It Pays

The audio files are split into six-minute intervals, and the pay is $10 per audio hour. They offer a bonus of $5 for every three hours of transcription completed each month.

When It Pays

You may transfer your earnings to your PayPal account anytime. There are no minimum withdrawal limits.

Where to Sign Up: https://scribie.com/

Transcription Company #5 – AccuTran Global

AccuTran Global, founded in 2002, is a full-service Canadian transcription company. They specialize in data entry, transcription, translation, and editing, plus financial and/or administrative support.

They hire home-based workers in the United States, Canada, and the United Kingdom.

Requirements:

- Type sixty words per minute (but seventy words per minute is preferred)
- Good listening skills
- Excellent English skills
- Internet research skills
- Ability to follow instructions
- Good communicator
- Background with knowledge in insurance, pharmaceuticals, electronics, real estate, and banking is preferred

Technical Requirements:

- Computer less than four years old
- Windows XP or newer
- Headphones
- Foot pedal

The busiest times are Tuesday through Thursday, 8:00 a.m. to 1:30 p.m., and Friday mornings.

What It Pays

The pay rate is $0.005 per word for basic audio and $0.006 per word for difficult and/or foreign audio. They offer a $50 bonus to those who make more than $2,000 within the first six months.

When It Pays

Payments are made on the fifteenth of the month by check or wire transfer.

Where to Sign Up: http://www.accutranglobal.com/

15. Make Money from Home as a Translator

As companies expand globally, more are reaching out to attract a wider customer base and are enlisting the assistance of efficient translators to do so. According to *Inc.*, $35 billion in revenue was generated from translation services.

Companies like LinkedIn recently connected with customers in China, while Facebook, Twitter, and Yahoo have stated their intention to reach global marketplaces as well. This, in itself, demonstrates that companies understand the importance of communicating with customers, of building a strong brand, and of engaging on a deeper level—and they're willing to do so by hiring translators.

If you are fluent in another language; can read, speak, comprehend, and write in that language at an advanced level; and have fast, accurate typing skills; then a translation gig might be the perfect opportunity for you. To enhance your chances of getting hired, you should become certified or accredited, practice your craft, gain experience, and get even more experience.

Although certification may not be required in your state, it almost always enhances your abilities to get hired. Many universities offer advanced degrees, language courses, and certification programs in translation. In addition, you can become certified with International Medical Interpreters Association or the American Translators Association. Once you have obtained this specialized training, you should take language proficiency tests, like the Defense Language Proficiency Test (DLPT), to demonstrate your skills. Next you must gain a bit of experience, so volunteer your services or find a paid internship where you can obtain references and samples.

As a translator, you'll work at language centers, hospitals, governmental entities, police stations, and more. Although most translators work on a freelance basis, you may find a part- or full-time position.

Here are some companies looking for work-at-home people to do translations:

Translation Company #1 – Verbalizeit

Verbalizeit makes it simple for businesses and individuals to cross the language barrier. This website offers translations for over 150 different languages, 140 countries, and various dialects. Sign up and tell them about your language experience and expertise. Then you must prove that you have the right skills to join their team. This will require some training and testing. After you have gone through that process, and you are accepted, it is time to start translating.

Requirements:

- Up-to-date computer or laptop
- Antivirus software
- Malware software
- Access to online thesaurus
- Access to online dictionary
- Access to online second language dictionary
- Spell-checker
- Grammar checker
- Microsoft Office with Word and Excel

You will be paid on the fifteenth and thirtieth of the month via PayPal, and the pay varies, depending on your skills. No mention is made of the exact amount they pay their translators. Your hours and days are flexible as long as you can make your deadlines for any jobs you have accepted.

Where to Sign Up: https://www.verbalizeit.com/english-english-transcription

Translation Company #2 – TextMaster

TextMaster was founded in 2011 and is a professional copywriting, proofreading, and translation service. They offer translations for ten languages: English, Chinese, Spanish, German, Portuguese, French, Dutch, Russian, and Polish. Set up an account similar to other freelancer sites and offer your services. Then apply for any writing, proofreading, or translation jobs that you are qualified to do. You will be tested on the skill you apply for. The pay is between $0.15–$1.40 per word, depending on the job. Once your account reaches $65, you can cash out via PayPal. Also a referral program exists where you will make 10% of your referrals' earnings for one year.

Requirements:

- Up-to-date computer or laptop
- Malware software
- Antivirus software
- Access to online thesaurus
- Access to online dictionary
- Access to Grammarly.com

Where to Sign Up: https://www.textmaster.com/

Translation Company #3 – Verilogue

Verilogue was founded in 2005 and wants to document a patient's history in a different way. Being a freelance translation typist at Verilogue means that you will:

- Transcribe material into the applicable language
- Transcribe material into English from an applicable language

What skills do you need?

- Be a native speaker of the applicable language
- Be advanced in English, in both written and oral communications
- Have previous medical transcription experience

You can log in to their system at any time as long as you can make your deadlines. You will receive $2.80 per audio minute for translating and transcribing, and $1.10 per audio minute for editing out the patient's personal information. For every quality control check on a transcript which you perform, you will be paid $1.20 per audio minute. Pay is done every two weeks by check or direct deposit.

Where to Sign Up: http://www.verilogue.com/company/careers

Translation Company #4 – Translators Town

Translators Town is a site that specializes in freelance translation jobs. The company is based in the United Kingdom, but jobs are open to everyone worldwide. No prior experience is required to work as a freelancer on this website.

There are a few membership options available:

- Free version – This version does not allow you to bid on jobs. Your name will be in their directory, and people can find you there and request you work for them. Unless you are an established translator, you will probably not get any invitations to work through this method.

- Standard version – This version costs around $75 per year. It does give you the ability to bid on jobs.

- Gold version – This version costs around $110 per year and gives you the ability to bid on jobs, just like the standard version. However, with this version, you can have a premium listing in the directory of translators.

Once you have won a bid and done the work, the client will then review your work, and you will get paid. Pay will depend on how much you bid on the job.

Where to Sign Up: http://www.translatorstown.com/

16. Make Money with Data Entry

Many opportunities exist to make money with data entry these days. Most data entry positions require a high school diploma or GED, accurate typing skills, basic computer skills, and an ability to follow instructions. You must also be organized and self-driven for these positions. The types of companies that hire remote data entry workers are elementary schools, government agencies, plus bookkeeping and payroll services. The amount of money paid for data entry will vary from company to company. Typically these companies pay through PayPal. Some may offer to send a check when a certain amount of money is in your account.

If you are interested in making money from home with flexible hours, check out the following companies online:

Data Entry Company #1 – VirtualBee

VirtualBee hires home-based workers to complete data entry jobs. Fill out their application, and, if you meet their requirements, you will be allowed to work for them. Log in to their system to start working on the available data entry projects. You are paid by check once you reach $30 in your account.

Data Entry Company #2 – Great American Opportunities

Great American Opportunities offers work-at-home opportunities for data entry on a seasonal basis. Send your résumé to tohair@gfundraising.com to apply for a position here. You must also take their data entry test, where they look for speed and accuracy. If you are accepted, you will be keying in names and addresses of people who have placed magazine orders. The pay averages from $0.10–$0.14 per form. The faster you type, the more money you make. Payments are made through direct deposit weekly. You can work anytime you want and will be considered an independent contractor.

Data Entry Company #3 – SigTrack

SigTrack offers data entry work on a seasonal basis. The data entry will include keying in information from petitions and updating voter registrations. You must be a US resident in order to apply for a position with them. After applying, you must pass a test on their site. If you fail the test, you can retake it; however, the number of times you can retake the test is limited. You must also verify your identity, done through Skype. They pay $0.037 per average petition signature to start and $0.15 for registration. Payments are made every Wednesday through PayPal. You choose when you work.

Data Entry Company #4 – Capital Typing

Capital Typing hires independent contractors to perform tasks such as transcription, data entry, translation, online customer support, market research, secretarial services, and editing. Contact the company about their application process.

Data Entry Company #5 – Dion Data Solutions

Dion Data Solutions hires home-contracted vendors for part-time data entry work. The company's motivation for hiring is to provide families in the United States an opportunity to make money from home with flexible hours. Qualifications for this job include a typing speed of at least 60 wpm, computer skills, multitasking, and excellent verbal and written communications skills. Dion Data only accepts applicants residing in the States. If working for this company, expect such data entry information as: medical claims, warranty cards, catalogs, mailing lists, surveys, and more. If you apply for a job and don't receive a response within ninety days, you can resubmit your application.

Additional tips to succeed at this type of position:

1. **Increase your typing skills.** Some great programs to check out are Typing Master, Type Faster, and Typing Trainer.

2. **Have a dedicated work space.** Set up a work space in which you can complete your data entry projects. This should include:

a) A desk and ergonomic chair.

b) A reliable computer.

c) A dedicated phone line.

d) Office software like Microsoft Office or Apache Open Office.

3. **Have a set schedule**. Set a schedule for when you will work. Do not do anything but data entry work during this set time.

4. **Rest often**. Take frequent breaks so that you don't overexert yourself.

Where to Sign Up:

VirtualBee - https://thesmartcrowd.lionbridge.com/

Great American Opportunities - http://gafundraising.com/

SigTrack - http://sigtrack.net/

Capital Typing - http://www.capitaltyping.com

Dion Data Solutions - http://www.diondatasolutions.net/opportunities.html

17. Make Money with Captioning Companies

Have you ever watched a subtitled television show, movie, or program? Ever wondered who was responsible for providing the text version of speech and other sounds available on DVDs, online videos, at theaters, and more? Well, captioners, of course!

Captioners are typically trained as court reporters and then venture out to captioning. They use special software and a stenotype machine with a phonetic keyboard to convert different types of audio content for display on a monitor, visual display system, or projection screen. This way, deaf and hearing-impaired individuals can read the text.

Being a captioner is a very specialized and fast-paced position! You need exceptional typing skills and must use a phonetic keyboard. Although it isn't required to get hired, you can become certified through NCRA (National Court Reporters Association).

There are two types of captioning jobs:

- **Real-time captioning** – For live video or audio of events, the most demanding of all transcription jobs. Most of the jobs for real-time captioning are done on location, but you can find a few opportunities for work-at-home positions.

- **Off-line captioning** – Previously recorded video or audio. You need knowledge of how to place the text and with the right timing.

Additional tips:

- Watch captions as much as possible, paying attention to real-time and off-line captioning.

- Decide upon a specialty, like TV captioning, and practice every day to enhance your skills.

- Always work at improving your accuracy.

- Build up your vocabulary and personal dictionary as soon as possible.

- Understand the field by staying abreast of the latest changes in the captioning industry.

- Join a well-known organization, like the NCRA, and take advantage of their tools and resources. Also they host special events that are great opportunities to network with other captioners.

Most captioning companies require experienced captioners, but a few companies are willing to give beginners a chance at a position. Below you will find some that offer work-at-home opportunities for captioning.

Captioning Company #1 – Aberdeen Captioning

Aberdeen Captioning is a family business located in California. They offer services to broadcasters and video producers. Most of their jobs are for in-house positions in Orange County, California; however, the jobs listed below are for work-at-home positions.

- **Real-time captioning** – They hire real-time captioning freelancers to provide captioning for live or live-to-tape programming. You must type 180–220 (stenographic) words per minute and have knowledge of Christian and Bible terminology. You will also need your own real-time captioning software, three phone lines, and a backup computer. It is possible to make up to $75 in this position.

- **Transcription** – Transcriptionists are hired to transcribe video clips. You must have transcription software, professional headphones, a foot pedal, and Windows Media Player. Also you need excellent grammar skills. This position pays $1–$1.50 per audio minute.

To apply for a position with this company, send your résumé and cover letter to info@abercap.com.

Captioning Company #2 – Caption Colorado

Caption Colorado provides closed-captioned services for things such as the news, live sporting events, feature films, webcasts, and educational programming. You are ready to apply here if you are:

- A writer with 98% accuracy
- A writer who accurately uses prefixes and suffixes
- A team player
- Reliable and punctual
- Self-correcting with a willingness to receive feedback

Selected applicants will be invited to take an assessment consisting of a thirty-minute new program. The assessment is scored on comprehensibility, completeness, accuracy, conflicts, and word boundary problems. The applicants with the top scores are interviewed and then the decision to hire will be made.

Where to Sign Up: http://captioncolorado.com/careers/

Captioning Company #3 – Rev.com

Rev.com offers three work-at-home opportunities for freelance workers: transcriptionist, captioner, and translator. Here you will choose your own work schedule. Work as little or as much as you want. You get to choose the projects you want to work on. You receive regular coaching and feedback on your work. Rev pays weekly through PayPal for all completed work.

Ranges of Pay

- Transcriptionist – $0.40–$0.65 per audio minute
- Captioner – $0.40–$0.75 per audio minute
- Translator – is $0.05–$0.07 per word

Where to Sign Up: https://www.rev.com/

18. Making Money With Rideshare Companies

Has your car ever broken down, and you needed to get a lift from someone fast? Has your ride ever flaked out on you and left you stranded? Have you ever wanted to leave a place but had to wait until the other members of your party were also willing to leave? Well, these types of situations happen to people every single day, and most of the time they are unable or unwilling to find a taxi and don't want the inconvenience of a bus or train. So they call a ridesharing company for help. Ridesharing is basically a higher-end taxi service that enables drivers and users to connect via a smartphone app using GPS functions. Vetted drivers use their own vehicles to pick up users and are paid a fee for their time. In turn, users can get from point A to point B conveniently.

So, if you like driving, and don't mind putting some wear and tear on your vehicle, working as a driver for a rideshare company might be the perfect opportunity for you. Uber and Lyft are two of the main leaders in the ridesharing industry.

Both companies are based in San Francisco, CA. Uber was founded in March of 2009 by Travis Kalanick and Garrett Camp. Lyft was founded three years later in June 2012 by Logan Green and John Zimmer. Uber's and Lyft's pricing models are nearly identical, and the services they provide to consumers are virtually indistinguishable. Where they are materially different is how they position themselves in the marketplace. Uber's slogan is "Your private driver," giving off more of a professional and corporate vibe, reminiscent of a chauffeur-driven car. Lyft, on the other hand, whose slogan is "Rides in minutes" has a bit more down-to-earth feel, as if you were catching a ride with a good friend.

Uber is currently valued at an eye-popping $68 billion dollars and available in more than five hundred cities and sixty countries worldwide. Lyft is currently servicing a little over 230 cities in the

States and nine international cities, with its latest valuation hovering around the $5.5 billion range.

Both companies can provide a fantastic opportunity for you to earn a part- or full-time income.

Rideshare Company #1 – Uber

At Uber, drivers use their own cars and work according to their own schedules. Passengers can request rides on the Uber app, and nearby drivers are alerted of a potential rideshare opportunity. One of the reasons Uber has become so big recently is it is usually far less expensive to hire an Uber driver than to use a taxi or limousine service.

How It Works

In order to get become an Uber driver, you must be over twenty-one and possess a clean driving record with no major accidents in recent years, no DUIs or too many tickets. In addition, you must have personal auto insurance and liability insurance that is covered by Uber. You must also have a smartphone and a four-door car manufactured in 2006 or a more recent model. Your car must pass an initial car inspection, and you must pass a criminal background check to ensure the safety of your passengers and the quality of your service.

Besides these basic requirements, drivers must do well on the Uber scoring system. This system allows passengers to leave feedback on their ride experience and rate the driver on a scale of one to five. It is imperative to maintain a good score, and Uber currently asks drivers to maintain an average score of 4.6 on their reviews.

To sign up, visit the Uber website and fill out the relevant forms and submit the details of a criminal background check plus your car inspection. Once all the formalities are fulfilled, you sign a contract with Uber to get started. The contract does not exclude you from working with other companies, and drivers are free to even work with a competitor, such as Lyft.

One of the biggest benefits of working with Uber is the ability to set your own schedule. This means flexibility and the ability to take time off with no notice or work as many hours as you like to earn more money.

When you're ready to pick up riders, you make your availability known through the Uber mobile app. Just turn it off when you don't want to work.

What It Pays

Uber drivers can make anywhere from $20–$30 an hour and tend to earn more than taxi drivers or chauffeurs.

Uber requires users to register with a credit card upon signing up and to pay for rides using that card. The whole process is made cash-free. The app tracks the earnings of its drivers, and payments are made on a weekly basis through direct deposit.

Where to Sign Up: http://ubr.to/2bCldhU

Rideshare Company #2 – Lyft

Lyft is quite similar to Uber and is a very reliable and professional ridesharing company. With Lyft, drivers must be twenty-one years of age or older and must possess a valid driver's license for the state where they intend to drive (and valid for at least one year). They must have a clean driving record and pass a criminal background check. Finally they must be insured on the vehicle they intend to drive.

Lyft vehicle requirements in most markets are that cars should be 2004 or more recent models.

All potential drivers must do a welcome ride with a Lyft mentor. These sessions include a car inspection, driver interview, and test-drive, ensuring an extra layer of screening for drivers. In order to do well on this session, watch all the welcome videos on the Lyft website and know how to operate the Lyft app. Also make sure your car is clean and presentable.

The sign-up process is simple, and you can do this on the Lyft website. If you've never driven for a rideshare website company before, you may want to know that Uber offers a bonus of $500 for drivers who have driven with Lyft first.

You can also get a sign-up bonus on Lyft by using another driver's referral code, which can be from a friend, or you can simply search for one online. You can also share your own referral code with friends to earn bonuses once you've started working with Lyft.

When It Pays

Drivers' earnings are paid on a weekly basis on every Wednesday.

How It Pays

Lyft drivers are paid via ACH bank deposit; therefore, a valid checking account is required. Lyft usually deducts a 20% commission on earnings; however, drivers can keep the full amount of their tips. Another advantage of using Lyft is that, the more you drive, the less of that 20% commission Lyft will deduct.

Where to Sign Up: http://lft.to/2b0kF6l

19. Get Paid to Run Errands

If driving people around isn't your thing, perhaps you'd prefer running errands instead. Not only is this opportunity fun but extremely lucrative too. Not convinced? Consider these facts:

The virtual assistant (VA)/personal assistant (PA) industry is predicted to be worth $5 billion by 2018. Businesses, entrepreneurs, and even stay-at-home parents are always looking for ways to save time. Because most are open to paying someone else to do the tasks for them, the PA business is booming.

As a PA, you will likely complete these tasks for your client: make and cancel appointments; contact businesses by phone to inquire about items and then pick them up or place an online order; make and revise travel arrangements; and so on.

With this in mind, many companies have entered this arena and are now hiring individuals, just like you, to do everyday tasks for people who need assistance. Unlike the tasks previously mentioned, these companies are looking for people to actually go somewhere to complete some miscellaneous task for the client.

Getting started as a PA is not difficult at all, but you must be willing to do the following:

- Hustle. Get things done that others aren't able to do (like running errands during work hours).

- Have dependable transportation so you can complete tasks timely.

- Be able to lift fifteen pounds or more (some tasks will require you to lift heavier items).

- Build a good reputation as someone who gets it done!

- Complete the tasks quickly and efficiently so you please the client and make more money.

- Know how to communicate properly with your client and your client's people. Remember, there may be times when you will be representing your client, so how you behave and speak will reflect back on your client.

Ready to get started? Here are a few companies looking to hire people to complete tasks for them and their clients:

Personal Errand Company #1 – TaskRabbit

This platform connects you to clients and has new tasks posted daily. The CEO, Stacy Brown-Philpot, used to work with Google and was named one of Fortune's 40 under 40. She launched TaskRabbit in 2008, available to taskers from the United States and London, offering a variety of tasks, from housework to making appointments to helping in a business.

To date, taskers number more than thirty thousand, and they make anywhere from $100 to $7,000 monthly, depending on the tasks they take on and the frequency of their tasks. Based on the numerous success stories of taskers, it is possible to quit your day job and do tasking full-time, especially if you have skills whereby you can charge by the hour.

Where to Sign Up: https://www.taskrabbit.com/become-a-tasker

Personal Errand Company #2 – Amazon Flex

You can make up to $25 an hour with Amazon Flex. This is a specific delivery-tasking service for Amazon and Prime Now customers. However, you must commit to the delivery schedule and must pay for your own car maintenance and fuel. Your earnings will depend on the delivery block that has a minimum of $36/block but can increase to $72/block, plus tips! You will need an Amazon account, and payout is done via Amazon's payout options.

Where to Sign Up: https://flex.amazon.com/

Personal Errand Company #3 – DoorDash

DoorDash is an on-demand food delivery service app launched for and by students of Stanford. As a DoorDash tasker, you will be known as a Dasher. All you need is to create an account, and have a mobile phone and Internet access. You must also be eighteen years old or older with one year of driving experience and a valid driver's license, clean driver's history, and insurance. DoorDash, however, also provides commercial insurance for its Dashers of up to $1 million for property damage or bodily injuries sustained during a delivery. Payments for work done are made weekly and are based on the number of deliveries made. They charge a flat delivery rate to their customers and pay you $25/hour, plus you get to keep your tips! Payouts are done via direct deposit.

With DoorDash, you are competing with other Dashers to get the delivery job so the Dashers who respond first get it. Once a delivery order is posted, you have only sixty seconds to respond. This means you must be on your phone and connected at the time you promised you would be online. Dashers who live near restaurants and busy areas tend to get more jobs than those who live farther away.

Just recently DoorDash started a pilot program for delivery of alcohol in Southern California. Last year, it partnered with 7-Eleven to deliver their products as well. For alcohol deliveries, the Dasher has to be at least twenty-one years old.

Where to Sign Up: http://bit.ly/2bClwcx

Personal Errand Company #4 – Instacart

Instacart, founded in 2012, is a grocery delivery service from selected establishments like Whole Foods and Costco. Called Shoppers, Instacart taskers have an hour to deliver the goods. As of 2015, four thousand Shoppers were in fifteen cities.

You can apply for four positions with Instacart: Shopper, Cashier, Driver, or Driver/Shopper. As a Shopper or Cashier, you don't need a vehicle but are limited to twenty-nine hours weekly because you are considered a part-time employee. As a Driver or Driver/Shopper, you are considered as an independent contractor and can work unlimited hours. However, you must provide your own vehicle.

To get started with Instacart, apply online to set up your account, attend a one-hour face-to-face orientation, and agree to a background check.

Working with Instacart, you can potentially earn $25/hour. However, the company has a formula which computes actual earnings that incorporates the number of items in the shopping list and the number of orders per shift, so the $25/hour can drop to $10/hour. Shoppers who get good reviews tend to get more orders.

Some other requirements to be a Shopper are:

- Must be at least twenty-one in all areas, except Boston, where the age of eighteen is accepted
- Must be able to lift over thirty pounds, although applicants with disabilities are accepted
- Must be eligible to work in the country
- Must have a smartphone and Internet access

Where to Sign Up: https://www.instacart.com/

Personal Errand Company #5 – WeGoLook

WeGoLook is a fantastic business app because it found a loophole in the Internet e-commerce system and decided to plug it. Its more than 25,000 Lookers check on claims regarding physical products being sold online to verify their authenticity. It saves consumers a lot of time and headaches by avoiding scammers and fraudulent sales.

Before you can become a Looker, you must pass a background check and have the proper demeanor and a gadget so you can post the photos of the products for inspection. You can be upgraded to Pro-Looker, which is for professionals and experts in specific fields. For this level, you become a badged Looker, get insurance, and pass a more stringent background and previous employment check. There is also a position for military men and their spouses, who receive preferential treatment.

Payment at WeGoLook as a Looker starts at $3/job, but you can make as much as $200/job, depending on the complexity of each job. Payout is from two to four weeks later, through major credit or debit cards or PayPal.

Where to Sign Up: https://wegolook.com/

20. Make Money as a Search Engine Evaluator

Search engines are not perfect and need human input so that the developers can design better search algorithms for optimal search results. People who rate the relevancy of search results are called search engine evaluators. They basically use their knowledge of language, culture, events, and news to evaluate and improve searches.

For instance, let's say an Internet user is searching for a Hilton hotel in Paris, but the search results instead yield events about Paris Hilton, the American actress, entrepreneur, and socialite. Well, you'd be pretty ticked off if you came across those unrelated results. Fortunately a search engine evaluator would determine that the results were faulty and would work to remove them before the end-user found them. Basically they'd use their human "search superpowers" to save the day.

As a search engine evaluator, you'd be hired by companies as an independent contractor to evaluate results using set search criteria. You would then interpret those results to see if the information was relevant. So, if you are Internet savvy, are knowledgeable about many topics, have strong analytical skills, and are up-to-date on current events, trending topics, pop culture, and news, you may be the perfect candidate to be a search engine evaluator.

With this position, you will work from home—as little or as often as you want. Some companies may require that you work certain days, which will be disclosed when you apply for a position with them. However, you usually must work a minimum amount of hours per month to stay enrolled. Check each website for more on that.

Additional Tips for Succeeding as a Search Engine Evaluator:

- Take frequent breaks to avoid eye strain.

- You'll need fast-speed Internet, a smartphone, an ergonomic chair, desk, and a large computer screen.

- The projects may be sporadic so you'll need multiple streams of income to ensure that you're prepared for any dry spells.

The companies below are just a few that hire search engine evaluators.

Search Engine Evaluator Company #1 – Appen

Appen is an award-winning company that helps other companies expand into the global market. Appen not only hires search engine evaluators but is also an expert in translation. Appen hires people for translation, transcription, and linguist services. Recently the company has even expanded into social media evaluations to improve the news feeds of large tech companies. To work as a search engine evaluator with this company, you must be available part-time, typically five hours a day, Monday through Friday. You must also go through training before you begin earning money. The training consists of practice ratings and a test. Once you meet their standards, you will start getting paid. Search engine evaluators earn between $13 and $15 dollars an hour.

Requirements:

- Interest in surfing the Internet

- Basic skills for installing software

- Experience with web browsers

- Up-to-date knowledge on culture, news, media, business, and sports

- Flexibility in schedule

- Willingness to ask questions

- Strong attention to detail

- Working well solo

- Excellent English, both spoken and written
- Excellent communication skills
- Laptop or desktop
- High-speed Internet connection

Before you apply for a position, completely read the description and requirements before you apply. You will be paid once a month through PayPal or direct deposit.

Where to Sign Up: http://appen.com/company/opportunities/

Search Engine Evaluator Company #2 – Leapforce

Leapforce is an established search engine company that hires people to work for them around the globe. Like Appen, Leapforce is great for bilingual candidates as the company hires for multiple languages. Leapforce recently added a new position called Personalized Search Engine Evaluator. If you are interested in this position, you must be an active Google user, which means using Gmail, Google+, and Google Play.

You are given tasks based on your personal use of your Gmail account. You should be using Google at least once a week. You will also need good analytical skills and reasoning abilities. Once you apply for the position, you must take and pass a three-part exam. It will test your skills on a practical level, plus your comprehension and theoretical abilities. In addition, it will evaluate how likely you are to succeed at the search engine evaluation process. The test is difficult, and you can only retake the exam one time.

There are no fees to join Leapforce, and you will be paid once a month through direct deposit within thirty days of receipt of a valid invoice. You are paid per task and have a time limit to complete those tasks. It is possible to earn around $13.50 per hour.

Where to Sign Up:
https://www.leapforceathome.com/qrp/public/jobs/list

Search Engine Evaluator Company #3 – iSoftStone

Based in China, iSoftStone was founded in 2001 and hires individuals for long-term projects. Most gigs involve rating the relevancy of ads or landing pages. In addition, you may rank keywords and website queries to determine if the search results are relevant. At iSoftStone, you typically work with the Bing search engine. You will be considered an independent contractor and not an employee of the company. This means that you are responsible for paying any and all taxes on what you earn.

You can log in and work whenever you want, but you are required to work at least ten hours a week and are limited to twenty-five hours maximum. You must be at least eighteen years old and a US resident. You must also complete training, pass a test, have high-speed Internet, a Windows-based computer, and be a native speaker with excellent grammar.

As a search engine evaluator, you can earn $13 per hour and will be paid once a month through either PayPal or direct deposit. If you can consistently work over thirty hours a week and have a high accuracy rating, you can make $14 or more per hour. Typically the higher hourly rates are reserved for individuals with exemplary accuracy ratings.

Training includes studying a seventy-plus-page document and then answering questions about an ad rating. If you don't pass, you can retake the exam.

Where to Sign Up: https://issworld.isoftstone.com/

Search Engine Evaluator Company #4 – ZeroChaos

Out of all the search engine evaluator companies, ZeroChaos hires US individuals as employees and pays the highest hourly rate of $15 an hour. However, they do not pay benefits, and their part-time employees typically have a university degree or professional experience. The employees also possess excellent writing, comprehension, analytical, and research skills, plus are familiar with media, web culture, and social culture. As an Ads Quality Rater, you'll need high-speed Internet and a smartphone (iPhone, Android, or Windows based). Basically you will work diligently to improve the accuracy of webpage ads. If hired, you'll be required to work a minimum of ten hours a week but less than twenty-nine. These hours are flexible, according to your own schedule.

Where to Sign Up: http://www.zerochaos.com/careers.php

21. Get Paid to Take Surveys

If you like to share your opinions with others, then you may want to give online surveys a try. This is a great way to make a little extra cash, and hundreds of companies enlist users to complete surveys online. It is possible to make $50–$100 per month in cash or free products for taking just a few surveys. Below we will discuss a few of the websites where you can make money for taking surveys.

Survey Company #1 – Opinion Outpost

Opinion Outpost connects major businesses and corporations to their customers. The input they receive from users completing surveys helps businesses serve their customers better. Members of this site can earn cash or gift cards, and they are automatically entered into Opinion Outpost's quarterly $10,000 prize drawing.

When creating an account at this website, provide your name, email address, and gender. Read and agree to both the Privacy Policy and the Terms and Conditions. After completing your registration, you will be sent an email invite. You must then finish a short sign-up process before you begin. This process will help find the best fit for you.

As you take surveys, you will earn points, which can then be redeemed for cash (through PayPal) or gift cards. Every two hundred points equals $20.

Where to Sign Up: https://www.opinionoutpost.com/

Survey Company #2 – Pinecone Research

Pinecone Research also connects businesses with its customers; however, it is an invitation-only survey panel, and you must be invited by a current member or find a Join link posted on their website.

This website is open to Americans, Canadians, Germans, and those living in the United Kingdom. Once you become a panelist for this company, you will be paid $3.00 for every survey you complete. You can receive payment through PayPal or select other rewards from an extensive catalog.

Where to Sign Up: https://www.pineconeresearch.com/

Survey Company #3 – GlobalTestMarket

GlobalTestMarket gives users an opportunity to directly influence global market research. The website has partnered with top companies from around the world. The company was founded in 1999 and has over 1,400 clients in sixty countries.

Sign up for free to be a member of this website. You will receive surveys about movies, automobiles, consumer products, restaurants, current events, and more. You will be awarded MarketPoints, as well as given sweepstakes entries. The MarketPoints will expire if not used in three years—or in twelve months if the account is inactive. Each 1,200 points equals $50. You can receive payment through PayPal, check, and gift cards.

Where to Sign Up: https://www.globaltestmarket.com/

Survey Company #4 – Vindale Research

Vindale Research was founded in 2005 and is an online market research panel. They have paid out more than $5 million dollars to people who have participated in surveys on brands such as Amazon, Netflix, and Disney. Surveys may require you to purchase products, but you are free to skip those if you do not want to participate in them.

First thing, sign up for a free account. Remember to fill out your profile completely to increase your chances of qualifying for special surveys. Once you have done so, you will have access to all the ways you can earn money through this website. You are free to take as many surveys as you wish in one day. There is no threshold. You must have $50 in your account before you can request payment.

Where to Sign Up: https://www.vindale.com/v/index.jsp

Survey Company #5 – Toluna

Toluna was created in 2000 and offers real-time digital consumer insights. They have nineteen offices spread over Europe, North America, and Asia Pacific. Toluna has a voting community of ten million members across fifty-seven countries.

You will be paid approximately $1.50 for each survey, on a reward system, so you will earn points. Each ninety thousand points is equal to a $30 PayPal e-certificate. They also have apps that you can use on your Android or Apple mobile devices. This means that anytime you have a free moment, you can access surveys and make money. To start an account is free; all you need is an active email address.

Before you decide to register with one of the other survey sites either listed here or found through an Internet search, beware. Not every company is genuine. A lot of Internet sites are scams and will not pay for the surveys that you have completed. It is worth the time to find out as much information on the site as possible before you decide to give it your time.

Where to Sign Up: https://us.toluna.com/

22. Making Money from Selling Stuff

Looking for a really great and easy way to make active income? Consider selling your unwanted items for cash. If you're like me, you probably have all sorts of interesting items that you just had to have at one time but can no longer use. Perhaps it's in your garage or stuffed somewhere in your closet or crawl space. Either way, it is taking up valuable room in your home, condo, or apartment, and it is now time for you to pass it on to someone else. After all, one man's junk is another man's treasure.

The good news is that you don't need to set up a garage sale or take your goods to a consignment shop. You can sell them by using eBay, Amazon, or Craigslist. In some instances, you won't even leave home. Sounds amazing, right?

Here's how to get started:

eBay

The eBay idea started in 1995 in the living room of Pierre Omidyar in San Jose. The website was set up so that individuals could sell goods or services under a person-to-person arrangement while at the same time connecting with others and providing feedback and reviews.

Everyone jumped on the eBay bandwagon because it bypassed traditional middlemen and traders to became the go-to place for hard-to-find objects. Most items were sold at a discount, and some savvy sellers even offered free shipping. In the past, bidding was fun and free of charge. For sellers, the first fifty listings were free, after which vendors were charged corresponding fees: the $0.30 minimum for ad insertion and the 10% fee on the final sales price. Now eBay charges $3 for ads where the reserve price is $0.01–$149.99 and a 2% commission off the reserve price for items that are $150 or more. Although this is a price increase, buyers and sellers are still flocking to eBay to make transactions.

As of January 2016, eBay has 162 million users and twenty-five million sellers. Last year, sellers sold merchandise and services worth over $82 million. Based on a 2014 report, every hour, eleven million users are searching for something on eBay.

The exciting prospect about eBay can be found in the numbers. Just look at the ratio between buyers and sellers—162:25. A huge income opportunity can be found here, folks!

How It Works

To get started selling items on eBay, go to www.ebay.com and create an account. This account can be linked to your PayPal account so that you can receive easy and fast payments whenever someone makes a purchase. Then go to My eBay and click on the Sell an Item tab. You will be taken through each and every step needed so that you can sell your stuff.

There are other small sellers' fees if you want to enhance and market your products or services more aggressively, but these fees are also minimal and have a maximum cap. You don't need any kind of fancy design in your placement ads; simply add words like "*WOW!*" and "*Great Deal*" on your product description. You set the amount you'd like the bidding to start at, and, if you want to receive a certain amount for an item, you can set a reserve. Then you wait for hungry eBayers to come along and bid on your listings.

How It Pays

Buyers can pay you via PayPal, PayPal Credit, check, or money orders.

Note: Check or money order payments are restricted and only allowed in certain categories. Click here to view accepted categories.

When It Pays

You are paid whenever someone purchases the item you're selling.

Quick-Selling Strategies

- ✓ Decide right away on whether to open a personal account or a business account. The difference between these two accounts can be found in the benefits and fees. For instance, the private eBay account is aimed at buyers who want to sell a few items that belong to them personally. For example, if your aim is to just clear out your attic of the items that you no longer want, then a private account would work best for you. However, if your aim is to start and run a business on eBay where you sell over $250 worth of items a month, or plan to become an eBay trading assistant, or plan on creating items and selling them on eBay, then you need a business account.

- ✓ Spend time selecting your eBay username. You should focus on something easy to remember and avoid anything which may be offensive to anyone. Also, eBay has guidelines on usernames with which you should be familiar. On the other hand, if you're stuck and can't seem to settle on an easy-to-market and an easy-to-remember username, no worries! Use something temporary. You are allowed to change your username later on, although it would be highly recommended to do so before you go full blast with your marketing. Avoid frequent name changes because this will not help you build a good seller's reputation.

- ✓ Open a PayPal account because this is the simplest and quickest way to get paid. A good idea would be to set up a personal PayPal account rather than a business PayPal account because, as a business vendor, PayPal charges a fee of 2.9% plus $0.30 on every transaction for local sales. You can always upgrade once your business gets off the ground.

- ✓ If you're a stickler for privacy, get a P.O. Box because, when you are shipping items, you will be required to provide a return address.

- ✓ Get supplies for packaging before you start listing anything. If you buy these wholesale, you save more. Just don't overspend on supplies. Also, knowing the dimensions and weight of your packages to be shipped will give you more accurate shipping rates, so you can incorporate the rate into your selling price, then offer free shipping. Also be sure to check shipping costs for heavy items (those weighing over fifty pounds).

- ✓ Check prices of other similar items before selling yours. When you browse on eBay, you will notice many items priced ridiculously low. Don't give in to a price war temptation with these sellers. Find reasons to ask for a higher price for your item based on its features, because, after all your effort, selling for a dollar will just not make you any money—unless the item is worth $0.10!

- ✓ Offer discounts to enhance bids.

- ✓ Understand the power of arbitrage. This is when you become a middleman and sell items from one website to your eBay customers while making a nice profit. It's like buying an item on Amazon to sell on eBay. You don't actually buy the item until you have sold it on eBay. The risk here is loss in profit, like, if the Amazon price increases, and you have not adjusted your eBay price. Or even worse, loss of business reputation should the product be out of stock and you have no other source.

Where to Sign Up: http://www.ebay.com

Craigslist

Craigslist was introduced in the late 1990s and is categorized as an online classified ad website where a person can go to find jobs, large and small items for sale, and services. It is now used by people from seventy different countries with an average of fifty billion views monthly. Contrary to popular belief, Craigslist is not entirely free advertising. Some fees can be levied on your ads. For example, you can be charged up to $75 for job postings and $10 for brokered apartment rentals. The exact rate would depend on the location where you're placing the ad.

People seem to really enjoy placing ads on Craigslist. As of the end of 2015, sixty million users were on Craigslist with around eighty million ads. If you're considering selling items on Craigslist, you can make a lot of money. All sorts of items—from electronics to books to everything in between—can be sold on Craigslist.

However, Craigslist forbids the sale of some items and services. For instance, they forbid you to sell items that may sicken or harm the recipient; no sales allowed of live animals, insects; etc. You are also prevented from selling counterfeit or illegal items or any obtained during crimes, plus controlled products (alcohol, tobacco, prescription drugs, medical devices, lottery tickets, etc.). They also forbid you to sell airfare or travel vouchers, or government benefits, such as food stamps, etc. For more detailed information on what is allowed and what is not, click here.

How It Works

To sell items on Craigslist, you simply go to Craigslist and create an account. Find your geographic area and follow the instructions to list your items for sale. Be sure to include the amount you'd like to receive (and, on larger items, leave room for the buyer to negotiate with you). Then wait for emails to come in, requesting to buy your item.

Quick Selling Tips:

- ✓ Understand that users of Craigslist are looking for a bargain. Listing items priced way above their average price range is just a waste of time.

- ✓ Craigslist is great for local sales, so use this as your guide when picking products or services to advertise.

- ✓ Never agree to a noncash transaction, such as a check. These can bounce, and credit cards can be denied, after the seller has the item. In addition it's best not to hold an item for a customer. Practice the policy of "first buyer with the cash gets the item."

- ✓ Craigslist has its share of scams and bad reviews. To protect you, keep your personal information private. Never give out your phone number or address, or meet buyers at or in your house. Agree to an online transaction or arrange for a meeting in a public place. Some police stations have begun to set aside staging areas for just this purpose, so check out your local law enforcement department.

- ✓ Install the Craigslist app so you can always monitor your ads.

- ✓ Expect buyers to barter and to not be satisfied unless they get some discount, so adjust your pricing a little in anticipation of this.

- ✓ Don't be afraid to say no if you feel the asking price is just too low.

- ✓ Be honest when advertising. By doing this, you build a good reputation and can rely on word-of-mouth advertising.

Where to Sign Up: http://craigslist.org/

23. Making Money by Drop-Shipping

Trading—everybody loves trading items for other items. It is the lifeblood of many entrepreneurs and has been around since ancient times. It's buying and selling—and now that we're in the twenty-first century, it's even hotter and more lucrative than ever!

You can make some serious active income by drop-shipping products that people want, without even taking hold of the physical item. No more stacking boxes and boxes of whatever gadget you plan on selling. Now you can simply collect your customer orders and shipment details, and transfer them to your business partner (another retailer, wholesaler, manufacturer, or someone else), and they'll do all the dirty work of shipping the goods to the customer while you get paid for orchestrating the deal.

Does this sound like fun? You bet it does. People are making tremendous amounts of money every day from drop-shipping, and you can too.

Here are some tips to get you started:

First, you need a great product, not easily available in the market or something you can get at a very cheap price compared to the standard market price. Consider today's US souvenir and gift supply industry. Its annual revenue is estimated at over $17 billion. The demand is tremendous, and small companies can easily compete with large multinationals because the name of the game is something unique and appealing—which covers such a wide market! In choosing a product, you should keep the following tips in mind:

- ✓ Get a product that provides value.
- ✓ Know who you will market the product to; research the demand.

✓ Find a product that isn't a one-time wonder but something that can be used multiple times and be a staple for consumers so you have a higher chance of repeat sales.

Second, you need a dependable supplier. It's one thing to have a sellable product but another thing to have one which is well-made and which can be delivered in steady supply. With the first scenario, you won't enjoy sustained income because of spotty deliveries and inferior quality.

Third, you need a responsible drop-shipper. It's not enough to have a great product; the person with the great product should also be a trustworthy drop-shipper. Quite a number of companies engage in drop-shipping. Some of the key tips on spotting an iffy drop-shipper are:

- They charge ongoing monthly fees. You should not pay just for the opportunity to buy from someone.

- They are retailers, which means they will be competing with you. Look for someone engaged in wholesale only.

- You cannot confirm their land-based presence. No contact details are provided.

- They do not speak proper English, which is not necessarily a problem but carries some risks in communication.

- They do not reply to your inquiries in a proper, timely manner. This suggests an amateur operation that may leave you hanging high and dry when you need them.

Fourth, ask about terms. Many drop-shippers have a minimum order volume requirement and charge a basic shipping fee. Make it a point to know these and other pertinent information before you start marketing. You must incorporate these fees into your pricing so you don't end up working for pennies.

Fifth, prepare your start-up capital. This kind of income opportunity requires an initial investment. The good news is that the exact amount would depend on your discretion in choosing a product to market. If you choose a high-end product, you will require more start-up capital because you must first buy those products.

Sixth, don't limit your choices to local suppliers. Think global. However, keep in mind that international supplier partners might charge international shipping charges. Plus, foreign exchange rates on currency are subject to fluctuations, which may eat into your profits.

One such international commerce website is Alibaba, a Chinese website engaged in e-commerce for small to large businesses plus individuals. Last year, on Singles Day, Alibaba sold merchandise worth $1 billion in just eight minutes before lunch! By the end of the day, the website had sales of $14.3 billion.

People are looking for new and interesting products on the Internet. They would rather stay home than brave traffic or deal with grumpy sales people. Online sales are expected to continue their upward trajectory with no significant downturn anytime soon.

24. Winning with Amazon's FBA (Fulfillment by Amazon) Program

If drop-shipping isn't your thing, you can try Amazon's FBA program. It is one of the most advanced fulfillment networks in the world. With this program, sellers can store their new or used items in Amazon's Fulfillment Centers and then sell them on Amazon without being worried about the hassles of taking orders, payments, customer fulfillment, or returns.

Think about it. You can handpick the items you want to sell and then ship them to Amazon to do the rest. With Amazon FBA, you are truly spoiled and taken care of, almost like a privileged VIP vendor. For instance, no heavy data uploading is necessary, as the logistics of processing and delivering are handled by Amazon! How could you not love this program?

Everything you need to know about using Amazon FBA:

1. Decide whether you will use your account as a professional or a personal seller account and sign up for the program. The monthly subscription fee for the professional account is $39.99 a month and enables you to list as many items as you want. If you choose the personal account, you don't pay this monthly fee, but you can only list items that are $10,000 or less. In addition, you will be charged a $0.99-per-item fee for each item that sells. Keep in mind that these fees do not include the fees that Amazon collects for shipping, gift wrapping, etc. Amazon collects the payment from the buyer and then deducts its applicable per-item minimum referral fee and any applicable taxes and closing fees as well. Note: The professional account is good for sellers who plan to sell a higher volume of products.

2. Download the Profit Bandit app because this app will help you assess the products you choose to put on Amazon. A monthly maintenance fee for the app is $9.99. If you don't want to

spend money on this app, get the free Amazon app for sellers, although it still has some kinks in the system.

3. Find a product to sell. It doesn't even have to be something you make. You can get products from local retailers or crafters whom you trust, and whose quality and supply are reliable.

4. List the product on Amazon with your price.

5. Ship your product inventory to Amazon.

6. You can now start marketing them yourself or let Amazon do the marketing for you. Amazon will take care of packing, collecting, and shipping. All you do is wait for Amazon to forward payment to you, minus their processing fee.

7. Replenish your stock with Amazon and start the cycle all over again.

Quick Tips

✓ The first month you use Amazon FBA is currently free so it's a fantastic offer!

✓ Have at least $200 start-up capital to buy the products you want on Amazon. The average ROIs with this program is 50% to 100%, and it can be yours within a few weeks.

✓ Pick the right products by scouting around shopping malls, groceries, retail stores, and social media. Don't be hasty in your product selection. Take your time and get feedback from people you know.

✓ Don't limit your options to brand-new items. You can sell well-loved antiques, thrift items, wholesale items, one-of-a-kind items, books, your own product, vintage clothing. There are no boundaries except illegal stuff, of course!

✓ If you plan to sell more than forty items per month, you would be better off signing up for the professional seller's account that has more benefits. For example, with the professional seller's account, you can create new product listing pages; use third-party services, like Scoutify, Repricers, and Inventory

- Lab; have access to more seller reports; apply to sell in restricted categories; and more.

- ✓ You can upgrade your account from an individual seller account to a professional seller account whenever you like. However, the first month is free, so it may be wise to try out the professional account for at least that first month.

- ✓ Compute your profit margin properly. A 35% margin is fair, although you can simply give yourself a $5 profit minimum for every product and increase that amount accordingly.

- ✓ Pick the right category on Amazon to sell your product.

- ✓ Make your rules and be firm. Do not give in to price swings just to sell. If you believe in your choices, the buyers are out there. Wait at least three months before lowering prices.

- ✓ Pack your products well, especially if they can be easily damaged in transit.

Advanced Tip

- ✓ Don't have any unwanted stuff? Here's a great and sneaky trick: ask friends and family members to give you items that they no longer want. Or you can visit community-based organizations, like Freecycle Network, and sell those items.

When It Pays

Payouts are twice a month.

How It Pays

The FBA program sends payments to the seller's valid checking account. It can't be sent to another party.

The Amazon FBA program is easy, and it's so simple! Get your Amazon FBA Account now and start earning without having to quit your day job.

Where to Sign Up: https://services.amazon.com/fulfillment-by-amazon/benefits.htm

25. How To Make Money Selling Children's Used Clothing

Selling children's gently used clothing is a great opportunity to make extra money. You can do this in various ways. Many websites and smartphone apps are available. Below we will discuss some of these which sell children's used clothing, along with a few other ideas.

Children's Clothing Consignment #1 – Poshmark

Poshmark is a marketplace for selling women's, men's, and kid's accessories and clothing. The items listed on the site should be in good condition and clean. The descriptions of the clothing or accessories must be accurate and clearly represented. As a member, you are not allowed to sell fakes or replicas of any kind. Poshmark is only available to those living in the United States or its territories.

To get started selling your clothing or accessories on Poshmark, you will need to:

- Create an account.
- Start your boutique. You can list an item for sale in less than sixty seconds using the Apple or Android app (free to download).

After you have created an account, you will have your very own webpage that you can promote and share to bring attention to the items you have for sale.

Tips for selling your items:

- Confirm that your pictures are clear.
- Be sure to list and include pictures of any excessive wear, stains, or damage to the item.
- Write a thorough description of the item.
- Share your listing through social media.

- Join Posh Parties.

Poshmark does charge a commission of $2.95 on sales under $15. For sales over $15, they charge a 20% commission fee. Once the item has been delivered to the buyer, your earnings will be added to your account. You can either spend your earnings through the app or withdraw your money at any time.

Children's Clothing Consignment #2 – thredUP

Check out thredUP, a clothing consignment website that allows users to order a kit to send in their gently used women's, juniors', and kids' clothing. The clothing should be in excellent condition and not have any pillings, holes, or stains, or they will not be accepted. Clothing should also be in season and on-trend.

Once you order your Clean-Out Kit, fill it and return it to them. Upon receipt of your bag of clothing, thredUP can take a month or more to process its contents. They will inspect each article of clothing, and, if the item meets their standards, they will then photograph and place the item for sale on their website.

You will be paid upfront for items listed under $60, and anything listed above $60 is paid to you after the item sales. You can choose to use the money you made to shop on the site or have the money sent to you through PayPal. It can take up to two weeks to process your PayPal payment.

Other ways to make money selling used children's clothing are:

- Local clothing exchanges – You can find stores near you that buy and sell used clothing.

- Garage sales – Although not the optimal place to sell clothing, you can make a couple bucks selling used clothing.

- Donating to Salvation Army or Goodwill – Even though these places do not pay you for your used clothing, you can use your donations as a tax deduction at the end of the year.

26. Selling Books for Cash

With the economy the way it is today, every dollar counts. Thousands of people have started to sell used books online as a second or third income. It is possible to earn $500–$5,000 per month selling used books online.

With more than twenty million college students enrolled across the United States, someone is always looking to lower their tuition costs. Buying used textbooks is just one way that a college student can do just that, as they are more affordable than new textbooks. Used textbooks may not look as nice as the new ones, but that does not change the contents. You can sell used textbooks at a few places online, which will be listed later in this section.

The amount of money you can make from selling textbooks depends on the age and type of textbook you are selling. Textbooks that have become scarce and are used for reference manuals can bring in hundreds of dollars. A great place to find used textbooks is on a university campus bulletin board.

Library book sales are also another great place to find used books. Most of the time, you can find books priced $0.25–$1.00 at these events, and turn around and resell them for $5.00–$300.00, depending on the book. Arrive at the sale early to get the best selection of books and don't forget to bring something to haul away all the books you intend to buy.

Other places to find large amount of books for cheap prices are:

- Garage sales
- Yard sales
- Estate sales
- Thrift stores

- Used book stores
- Newspaper classifieds
- Craigslist

All these places are great for finding used books still in great condition but priced cheaply.

Before going out to buy books, you may want to invest in a barcode reader, a compact flash socket scan card, and price look-up software. You can even use your smartphone to scan the barcode on books when you are out shopping. Real-time pricing means that you will get the most up-to-date pricing from Amazon. The only downside to using a smartphone is that, if the reception inside the building is bad, you will have a hard time gaining access to book prices. This is where having the barcode reader has it advantage.

Once you have enough used books to sell online, it is time to find a place to sell them. Below we will discuss some book-selling websites.

Used Online Bookstore #1 – Half.com

Sign up for a free membership, and then go to your account and click the Start Selling Now link. Here you must enter your credit card information, direct deposit information (to get paid), and the shipping methods that you will use. Selling on this site is only open to those who live in the United States. There is no charge to register or list items on Half.com. If you are already a seller on eBay, you can set it up that, whatever you list on Half.com, will also be listed on eBay at the same time. You will receive the money that you made by direct deposit on the fifteenth and last day of each month. Receiving the money could take up to seven days.

Where to Sign Up: http://www.half.com

Used Online Bookstore #2 – BookScouter.com

This is a website that can be used to sell textbooks and used books.

This site is free, and no registration is required. To start selling here, simply enter the book's ISBN number. You will then see several vendors who want to buy your book, and you will be taken to their website to complete the transaction. Once that is done, you will receive an email with options on how you wish to ship the item. Once the vendor receives your books, BookScouter will send you payment.

Where to Sign Up: http://www.bookscouter.com

Used Online Bookstore #3 – Amazon.com

To get started selling books on Amazon, create a seller account. You will be asked to provide an email address and basic contact information. After this is done, you will receive an email stating that your seller account has been created. You can choose between an individual account or a professional account. Keep in mind that the professional account has a $39.99 per month fee but no closing fee, while the individual account has a closing fee of $0.99. You must also enter a valid checking account number to receive payment.

To list your books for sale, enter the ISBN number into the search box and confirm that you have Books selected in the product category before clicking Start Selling. You can then set the price of your book. To get a good idea of what other books of the same type are selling for, you can look at other sellers' listings. List the condition of the book (new, like new, very good, and so on). You must then ship the books you listed to Amazon, and they will ship the items when sold.

Where to Sign Up: http://www.amazon.com

Used Online Bookstore #4 – ValoreBooks.com

This website allows students to buy or rent cheap textbooks from rental providers and sellers. Give them a list of the textbooks you wish to sell. After they receive the list, they will send you a price quote for your books. You can add as many items that you'd like to sell to your shopping cart and then check out to receive a quote. Then print out the free shipping label and packing slip, and take them to your local

FedEx or USPS location within fourteen days.

Your items should reach the warehouse within two to ten business days. They will then evaluate your items and send you an email to let you know if your items have been accepted or rejected. Once your items are accepted, you will receive payment within fourteen days. Checks will be mailed through USPS and take seven to fourteen business days to arrive, or you can have the funds put into PayPal within two to seven business days.

Where to Sign Up: http://www.valorebooks.com

Used Online Bookstore #5 – Chegg.com

This is another website to sell textbooks. You will instantly know how much your books are worth simply by entering the ISBN numbers into the Chegg.com's search bar. Once you know how much you will get for your books, print out your free shipping label, package the books, and take them to your local UPS store. After Chegg receives your books, it could take up to ten to fifteen days to receive payment.

Where to Sign Up: http://www.chegg.com

27. Get Paid to Tutor Online

Calling all bookworms, geniuses, and intelligent individuals (yes, I'm talking to you)! After all, you're reading this book, and I know you're one smart cookie!

Did you know that you could make the world a better place by educating others and getting paid for your efforts? Individuals who enjoy tutoring and sharing their in-depth knowledge with others are making a full- or part-time income with online tutoring.

Now, when you're just starting off as an online tutor, your income can vary a lot, depending on what types of sites you use to secure clients, your experience as a tutor, and your specialty subject. If you're new to the education sector and don't have much of an online reputation as a tutor, it may take time to get new clients. However, with effective marketing, excellent feedback from students, and perseverance, you can steadily increase your customer base and income. In fact, many tutors working only five to ten hours a month earn about $75–$150 a month, making $15 an hour. However, experienced tutors can easily make $150–$300 for the same amount of hours at $30 per hour. Plus you can earn this money right from the comforts of your own home. Doesn't that sound amazing?

When you work as an online tutor, you work directly with a student or a group of students. You help them with a set topic, likely for an hour or so. Most sessions are conducted directly from the site that hires you as a tutor.

Additional Tips for Getting Hired by Online Tutoring Companies:

- When taking a test in your chosen subject fields, don't be intimidated. Just do your best and choose subjects you know pretty well.
- Be prepared to tell why you want to be a tutor. During most interviews, you will be asked about your tutoring experience,

why you want to be a tutor, and what you think makes you an excellent candidate.

- Be knowledgeable about the tutoring company, subjects offered, what separates them from the competition, and what unique skills you can bring as an instructor. Be prepared to sell your skills and experience during the online screening process and interview.

- To increase your likelihood of being hired by prospective students, be short, clear, and concise in your explanation of who you are and what your strengths are. Think of it as an opportunity to sell yourself to busy shopping customers.

- Continue to learn more about what you may not have done so well with during the initial testing process. Many services will allow you to retest at some point. This will make your portfolio stronger.

Online tutoring can be a great sideline. Of course it's not for everyone, but many people find it enjoyable as well as profitable. By following the above tips, you can make the most out of your tutoring experience and help students in the process. What could be better than that?

Eduboard, Chegg, Wyzant, Varsity Tutors, and Tutor are some great sites to check out.

Tutoring Company #1 – Eduboard

Eduboard is a service designed to help students of all ages and grade levels complete their homework assignments. If you are a student in need of a tutor, when you arrive on the website, you will submit your information and wait for a reply from a qualified tutor. Once the tutor receives your question, the information is sent to you quickly in the form of an attachment. This can be a text file or in video file format. These options are the fastest and simplest ways to deliver information to the student.

To be a tutor for Eduboard, register and fill out their application. You will be directed to take an English test. Once approved, you will start taking tutoring orders through your account.

Where to Sign Up: http://eduboard.com/

Tutoring Company #2 – Chegg

Chegg offers multiple services, such as textbook rentals, tutoring, and test preparation. Chegg tutors pride themselves in breaking down difficult subject matters for students when they cannot understand their own teacher at school. Chegg tutors will also work hard to get you caught up in the midst of a fast-paced course when you are lagging behind. Chegg has a very high rate of positive feedback and is esteemed as a reliable tutoring service.

When signing up as a tutor, you will select your best subjects, so that students with needs in those areas can be sent your way. You will have the opportunity to work with middle school, high school, and college students, as well as other professionals. Once started, positive tutor feedback is very important for the credibility of Chegg Tutors.

Where to Sign Up: http://www.chegg.com

Tutoring Company #3 – Wyzant

Wyzant is a tutoring service that connects educators and experts to students searching to gain knowledge in a plethora of subject areas, ranging from math to English, and sports to music. Wyzant provides one-on-one instruction with students. A place to meet is agreed upon with the student prior to the initial consult so that conditions work well for everyone involved. Wyzant tutors choose their own rates. Wyzant is connected to the student's bank account and handles payment for you. The service takes a fee for each client you are paid for. If accepted as a tutor for Wyzant, having a strong profile with a proven ability in multiple subjects will help students gravitate to you.

Where to Sign Up: https://www.wyzant.com/

Tutoring Company #4 – Varsity Tutors

Varsity Tutors provides academic tutoring and test preparation services. They go through a rigorous screening process to find the perfect tutor for their students so that they have a personality match and the best qualified tutor for the particular subject. They are so serious about their tutoring services that they offer a money back guarantee. Varsity Tutors hires an elite group of tutors who must go through a tough interview process and a background check. They tutor in-person or online, and many of the tutors have attended top-tier universities. When applying, be sure to highlight any qualifications you have to give you a better shot at scoring a job with Varsity Tutors.

Where to Sign Up: http://www.varsitytutors.com

Tutoring Company #5 – Tutor.com

From the very beginning, Tutor guarantees better grades for students not doing well in school. Tutor is available 24/7. They employ professors, Ivy League teachers, doctors, and many more to assist in the toughest of subject areas. Sessions are personalized, tailored to the student's subject and question, and are one-on-one. Not only do they offer services for several subjects but they also help with test prep and AP material as well. Tutors will have access to all age and grade levels, all the way through adults. You are invited to apply if you are passionate about your subject material. A test will be administered to prove your proficiency.

Where to Sign Up: http://www.tutor.com

28. Making Money with Creativity

Are you right- or left-brained?

More creative people are called right-brained people. Left-brained folks are typically thought to be more analytical and logical. If you're one of these artsy right-brained types, like me, you can monetize that creativity in many ways, especially on the Internet.

As of January 2016, the creative industry in the United Kingdom is worth 84.1 billion pounds! This sector is growing at double the pace of their economy and has become Britain's most successful story to date, according to UK's then Minister of Culture Ed Vaizey.

It doesn't stop there.

In Hong Kong, the creative industry is one of the most dynamic in their country, while, in most countries across the globe, creative entrepreneurship has been tagged as a critical key to jobs and income opportunities in our modern age.

There are many ways to make money with your creativity, and some of these include creating websites, logos, posters; designing T-shirts, mugs, stationery, bags, shoes; making crafts; or taking photos—the choices are endless. You can even sell your artwork for cash.

Just to give you an idea of how much money you can make using your creativity, here are some fantastic stories:

- *Harvard Business Review* calls artists and other freelance creative entrepreneurs the "supertemps" because this group of highly skilled individuals is growing at a steady rate in the United States and earning a very decent income.

- Chris Austin from Vancouver has an Instagram account with eight thousand followers. Four years ago, he quit his day job because his art was selling like hotcakes, and now 25% of his income comes from his Instagram sales. He makes one art piece a day and sells them for anywhere between $100–$200, and, because he has many followers, most of his work gets sold within an hour of posting.

These people are not any different from you. You too can make money with your talent! All it takes is some guts, a little help with the marketing, and a lot of whatever it is that makes your creative juices flow.

Here are some creative ideas to get that money flowing into your bank account.

Make Money Selling Computers for Cash

Old computers are referred to as e-waste. Did you know that the country's trash consists of only 2% e-waste? However, this 2% contributes 70% to the total toxic waste of the country! Thus, selling your old computers for cash is not just a nifty idea to turn junk into cash, it is also environment-friendly because computers can be recycled under a materials recovery program.

Other interesting facts about e-waste:

- Electronic items contain gold and other precious metals.
- For every million laptops recycled, the country saves energy equal to the energy consumption of over 3,600 homes annually.
- Computers are junked because consumers buy a later model, rarely because the computer no longer functions.
- Last year Apple harvested over 2,200 pounds of gold, worth $40 million, from recycled devices.

Several companies are willing to accept your old computers in exchange for some cash because they know how to refurbish the unit and put it back on the market. They are also knowledgeable about how to dispose of the toxic parts that can no longer be used.

Some of these companies are:

Computer Selling Company #1 – NextWorth

NextWorth buys all kinds of electronic devices from laptops to mobile phones and tablets. They have a network of over half a million customers, although all sales are done through eBay. As a person selling a computer, you can deal directly with them and get paid via PayPal, check, or Target gift cards.

The turnaround time for payment is at least ten days because the computer has to be checked and inspected. To turn in your computer, you can ship it straight to the offices of NextWorth or drop it in your local Target store. If you do drop it off in the Target store, that means getting a Target gift card, not cash.

NextWorth has a good support system in place, and you can contact them through phone, email, or chat.

Where to Sign Up: http://www.nextworth.com

Computer Selling Company #2 – Gazelle

Gazelle accepts tablets and Mac computers. However, before a sale is finalized, each item goes through the company's thirty-point inspection. The basic functions of the computer or tablet must be in good working condition. Gazelle will not accept damaged and nonfunctioning computers.

With Gazelle, the amount to be paid is estimated when you submit the specs of your computer. However, the final amount will depend on the result of their inspection of the unit.

This company also gives you an option for payment: Amazon gift cards, check, or PayPal. The agreed-upon amount will be remitted to you within one week.

Where to Sign Up: https://www.gazelle.com/

Computer Selling Company #3 – Cash for Electronic Scrap USA

CJ Environmental, Inc. has been around for over forty years and is a member of Inc. 500—the fastest growing companies in the country. They pay in check, PayPal, or bank wire, and provide for free shipping

Active Income Streams

and insurance. The check is mailed to you within ten days of receiving your computer, and you can track your computer with a tracking number provided by the company. They do not have hidden charges, like appraisal fees or broker's commissions.

In addition to buying computers, they also buy computer parts. So, if you have a nonworking computer, but some of its parts are still functional, you can sell them to this company. They buy motherboards, hard drives, RAM, IC (integrated circuit) chips, and processors.

They will also pay you a referral commission for every customer you send their way. In fact, they encourage collecting from family and friends and shipping it all together to them for a bigger payout.

Where to Sign Up: http://cashforelectronicscrapusa.com/

Computer Selling Company #4 – US.WeBuy.com

CeX is the company that runs US.WeBuy.com, and it has been around since 1992. They are found in nine other countries besides the United States. CeX buys cheap, then turns around and sells your item for a profit. For instance, they will pay $165 for an iPad and then sell it for around $300 or buy your MacBook Air for $188 and sell it for $470. This system may seem lopsided in favor of US.WeBuy.com, but CeX assumes all the marketing, logistics, and inventory headaches, which explains the high markup.

The good news is that they pay quickly and through PayPal, check, or voucher from CeX. All items pass inspection, which means you must ship it to them. If your item is rejected, it can be shipped back to you, no charge, or you can ask them to recycle it for you. If the computer is not functional but has working parts, CeX will assess the parts that can be bought from you and negotiate for the sale of the parts instead. You must be at least eighteen to sell on CeX.

Where to Sign Up: http://www.US.WeBuy.com

Computer Selling Company #5 – Gadget Salvation

Based in Chicago, Gadget Salvation will pay you via check or PayPal for your computer. They also offer free shipping and have one of the best reputations in the industry. They offer higher pricing compared to other companies and have been recommended by experts like LifeHacker.

One issue you might have with Gadget Salvation is not finding the perfect fit when describing your computer. If this happens, the quoted estimate will change and could be lowered after inspection. The company does prefer getting a computer that looks slightly used or new. However, based on many reviews and feedback, the company is upfront and honest with an A rating from BBB.

Finally, if you reject the new price and want your computer back, you must pay for return shipping.

Where to Sign Up: https://www.gadgetsalvation.com/

29. Sell Your Artwork for Cash

Art is hot. In fact, the US art market increased by 4% from 2015, selling a record high of $27.3 billion! And this art not only includes fine arts, like fancy paintings, but also artsy crafts and other creative works. Online sales alone are worth $3.27 billion and expected to exceed $9.5 billion by 2020. Plus you can sell your art for as low as a few dollars to tens of thousands. The possibilities are endless.

The key to selling art is finding buyers, and the best way to do this is to find the right venue to display your art where the right buyers see it.

That said, here are some crafty items you could focus on:

- Self-expression art
- Landscape views
- Local art
- Animals and wildlife
- Abstracts

Just remember to create art for yourself. Avoid trying to fit into the "popular trend" and be bold about your creativity. If you put love into your work, it will be seen and appreciated by others, and they will buy!

Two great websites where you can sell your art are DeviantArt and Redbubble.

DeviantArt boasts as being the largest online art gallery and community. In fact, they have over thirty-eight million members and have been around since 2000. Their members upload as much as 160,000 artworks daily and earn a minimum of 20% of the selling price.

Redbubble has unique art as its come-on. Here you can find artists who create mobile phone cases, stickers, T-shirts, posters, calendars, duvet covers, bags, journals, leggings, scarves, metal print art, and a whole lot more.

Besides these two sites, you can also sell your art on:

1. Facebook or Instagram using Spreesy, which is a free app service that enables you to get paid for your art through PayPal.

2. ArtPal, which does not charge membership fees, will get you up to 100% of your selling price if based on print-on-demand. Otherwise, income is 95%, with a 5% commission for ArtPal. All your earnings are paid via PayPal.

3. ArtFinder, which has a global market and sells original art pieces, accepts all major credit cards and PayPal.

4. Folksy is a place to sell handmade crafts, and each item is charged a minimal listing fee of about $0.20. You get paid through your PayPal account.

5. Foundmyself does not charge you anything to sell your art on their site but simply requests a token donation from a successful sale, the amount of which would depend on what you as the artist thinks is a fair commission. In fact, any sale is a private transaction between you and your buyer.

Finally another option would be to build your own website using one of the user-friendly open-source e-commerce platforms. However, this route would mean more administrative and marketing work, plus time away from your art.

Where to Sign Up:

Deviant Art – http://www.deviantart.com

RedBubble – http://www.redbubble.com

Facebook – http://www.facebook.com

Instagram – http://www.instagram.com

ArtPal – http://www.artpal.com

Art Finder – http://www.artfinder.com

Folksy – http://www.folksy.com

Foundmyself – http://www.foundmyself.com/

30. Website Flipping For Cash

Have you ever heard of flipping houses? Plenty of millionaires have been made from this strategy. What you might not know, however, is that you can also make cash by flipping websites. Yes, as more and more folks become online entrepreneurs, websites become even more paramount to their success. Therefore, website flipping is a very lucrative business that not only allows entrepreneurs to have a stronger web presence but enables you to make some great cash too.

With website flipping, you follow the same success principles as house flipping. Basically you buy low, renovate/improve the property before turning it around and selling it for a higher price. To explain further, when you flip a website, you basically improve its ranking, content, and overall design. You may add features (like an online forum, shopping cart, affiliate links) or custom-designed items (like books or products). The possibilities are endless and so is the cash, folks.

There have been cases of a website being bought for $10 and sold for more than $1,000 after extensive work was done on it. I've done it, and so have other people I know or have heard of. For instance, one spectacular success story involves Dave Hermansen, who bought a site for $1,800 and sold it for $173,000 three years after renovating it.

If you have outstanding design, writing, or SEO skills (or can partner with someone who does), please read on.

Website flipping makes sense because:

- Thousands of people don't know how to build a website.
- Even more are searching for a way to break into e-commerce with the least amount of effort, even if they have to pay more.
- The demand is increasing for operational websites.

Simple Steps to Website Flipping

Website flipping can be narrowed down to just three steps:

1. Buy
2. Fix
3. Sell

The key is offering value or focusing the majority of your efforts on step 2. However, this does not mean you buy websites randomly. It's best to pick a site that has the best potential for ranking, revenues, and traffic. Part of what is involved in step 2 is redesigning the layout, and making sure it is technically sound and has all the components of a good website, including links to social platforms and high SEO potential.

How to Get Started

If this is something you have never done before, start by using your own website. Build it, fix it, and sell it. This will help you get some experience without the added pressure of buying a domain. If you have a blog, then you must focus on turning it into a profitable blog, using advertising, driving traffic, focusing on better keywords, and repairing any bad backlinks. In essence, you want to sell a site that is already making you money.

Quick Tips for Flipping Websites

- ✓ Look for growth potential.
- ✓ Accept your limitations, and don't overreach or be too ambitious.
- ✓ Learn how to analyze the potential and the potholes of a website for sale.
- ✓ Don't be intimidated.
- ✓ Ask for help when you're unsure.

Once you feel ready to start investing, here are a few websites you might be interested in working with:

Website Flipping Site #1 – Flippa

Flippa, an Australian-based website with offices in San Francisco, is probably the most popular website for flipping sites. They sell websites using the auction method, but only members can bid and buy. As a member, you get access to tutorials, tips, eBooks, special promotions, and free credits with Upwork (formerly oDesk). Members pay listing fees, and Flippa gets a percent of any sale made using the website, although the actual transaction is between the buyer and seller.

When buying or selling a website on Flippa, you get to choose from several convenient payment methods, like electronic transfer payments or escrow. The average price of a starter website is $100, while established websites can charge higher.

Where to Sign Up: http://www.flippa.com

Website Flipping Site #2 – Digital Point

Founded by Shawn Hogan and based in San Diego, Digital Point is another marketplace for websites; however, it has had its fair share of controversy, particularly legal problems pertaining to the site. This website has around 150,000 members and is ranked among the top one thousand globally.

Like Flippa, here are tons of resources for its members, although the site itself looks very cluttered, dull, and basic. Aside from websites, Digital Point allows members to transact other business, promote their business, learn new web design tricks, sell or buy ads, check analytics, socialize, and use the site to network. There is no charge to join Digital Point unless you sign up as a Premium Member. As a Premium Member, you get better deals through lower prices, although the website is keeping the terms of their Premium Membership confidential.

Perhaps the biggest issues you may have with this website are that they can't be tracked down except through Twitter, and they tend to engage in moderate spamming. Still, it is a great place to meet people in the industry, get backroom information and deals done, and earn some money. They use PayPal for their transactions.

Where to Sign Up: https://www.digitalpoint.com/

Website Flipping Site #3 – Warrior Forum

Warrior Forum is a digital marketplace forum where registered members are allowed to participate. Selling and buying are done through the threads. You also get to send in queries and answer questions using the different threads on the website. All transactions must pass through Warrior Payments, which charges a flat rate of 2%. Any offer placed on a thread must be exclusive to Warrior Forum and have something special about it, like a lower price, freebies, or bonuses. All other offers that do not fall under this criteria are automatically placed in the classified section.

As a seller, you must be ready to offer support in case your buyer needs help after the sale. You are also prohibited from using paid testimonials, spamming anyone, or linking to off-site reviews.

The other rules to buy and sell on this website pertain to acceptable behaviors, ethics, and procedures. The listing fee is $20, and the bump fee is $19.95. The starting price of a website is $100, and web services can also be offered at a starting price of $100.

Where to Sign Up: http://www.warriorforum.com/

Website Flipping Site #4 – Empire Flippers

This is a website broker, founded by Joe Magnotti and Justin Cooke. They claim to sell over 90% of all website listings within three months' time. Sign up as an Empire Flipper, after which the website will email you all the terms and conditions for being part of their community. They can also review your website (for a fee) and will help you market your website (also for a small fee). If sold, they take care of the logistics in transferring ownership. In short, they make it easy for you to flip sites as they take care of the details.

Other marketplaces for flipping websites are BuySellWebsite (charges $39 for a two-week listing), DealASite (free listing), and Website Broker **(charges $9.95 for ninety days).**

Where to Sign Up: https://empireflippers.com/

31. Sell Your Crafts for Cash

Etsy

If you enjoy making things with your own two hands, be it stylish T-shirts, unique jewelry, or even one-of-a-kind paintings, then Etsy can be a great place to profit from your passions. Etsy is an online marketplace where artisans of all skills and types can sell their products online.

How It Works

Setting up a shop on Etsy is incredibly easy. To get started, pick a name for your shop, design a unique and brandable banner (or have one created for you), add a clever marketing description of each product, and upload a profile picture.

You can sign up for free; however, the cost of listing an item for four months or until it is sold is $0.20. Etsy also retains 3.5% of the selling price. Understand that—depending on your marketing skills—products and turnaround time will vary. Some sellers are more successful than others on Etsy. In fact, some Etsy sellers make over six figures, whereas some are barely breaking even. Etsy is a competitive marketplace unlike any other; so, in order to do well on Etsy, sellers need to stand out by selling unique products to a wider selection of buyers using a more attractive visual platform.

There's no limit to what you can sell on Etsy, from bridal accessories to animal portraits, original works to vintage items that you find at yard sales and antique fairs. The possibilities are endless. If you've got talent, you can profit!

The site has built up quite a following, so you'll have a good chance of getting your products in front of the right audience if you market them effectively. Even better, if you're a designer, you can upload something that you could make (according to your customer's precise needs), and then sell it to buyers on a made-to-order basis. Plus, as it is completely customized, you can charger higher prices for one-of-a-kind originals. This works best for items that have a quick turnaround time or if you don't have a lot of storage space in your location. It also means you don't need inventory, but you can still make some extra cash.

If you already have some ideas in mind, get cracking. No need to stall. The time is now to create your very own Etsy store.

Advanced Selling Tips:

- **Study the market.** Before creating your products, it is best to study the market. Evaluate what items are hot and which ones are not. Ask people you know to evaluate your product ideas to see if they have marketability. Short list those ideas that have a wow factor.

- **Aesthetics matter.** Don't put out garbage. Although one man's junk may be someone else's treasure, that isn't necessarily the case on Etsy. Therefore, it is paramount that any item you create appears pretty to people! The nicer, more thought out, and well organized your storefront is, the more likely people will take a look around. Imagine you had an actual storefront. You wouldn't misspell signs or leave things on the floor, would you?

- **Establish a recognizable brand.** Treat your virtual storefront the same way. Make it nice, neat, and memorable. Differentiate yourself from other sellers.

- **Market yourself effectively**. Don't be afraid to market yourself, as you are your product. Your products are amazing, just like you, so be proud of the products you have made and market them effectively. Let people know that you sell quality products and stand behind your work.

- **Exceed expectations.** When someone buys something from you, they should get a special treat—fast service, exceptional quality, etc. After all, you are one-of-a-kind and so are your products, so why shouldn't the world see that in all its glory?

Where to Sign Up: http://www.etsy.com

32. Mystery Shopping for Cash

Mystery shopping can be a really great way to earn extra or part-time/full-time income. As a mystery shopper, you will basically visit department stores, hotels, car dealerships, restaurants, and other establishments to evaluate the target business's practices and quality of service you receive (called "shops" of various kinds). Companies hire mystery shoppers so they can get an insider's view of how employers are treating customers. In most instances, the employees won't know they're being mystery-shopped; however, on some occasions, you'll perform a revealed shop, and you'll inform the employees that they've been mystery-shopped (typically after they've been evaluated). You will then detail your findings in a comprehensive report for your client.

The amount of money you can make depends on the type of assignment and company you're working for. Some mystery shopping companies don't pay as much as others. Therefore, it makes sense to use more than one. In fact, most mystery shoppers are signed up with over fifty mystery shopping companies so they have access to a wide range of shopping opportunities. They then typically receive assignments from twenty or more.

To work as a mystery shopper, you don't need any specific training or education; however, you must be detail-oriented and organized, and have exceptional written and verbal communication skills. If you choose, you can become certified at MSPA (Mystery Shopping Providers Association). They provide certification to those individuals serious about pursuing a career as a mystery shopper. To them, having specific training and shopping standardized is crucial to succeeding at this profession.

The average part-time mystery shoppers make about $5,000 a year, but the average full-time mystery shopper makes over $52,000. This equates to most beginners making more than $8 per hour, while experienced shoppers are making $25 per hour. For shoppers who get paid by assignment, they make about $10–$100.

The assignments that offer more money are usually reserved for established shoppers, who consistently meet deadlines and complete reports in a timely manner. In addition, the higher-end restaurant and hotel mystery shops typically require that you have previous mystery shopping experience.

Most assignments take between fifteen minutes to an hour to complete. However, you must allocate some time to completing reports, depending on their complexity.

You will, on occasion, be reimbursed for food or other items you purchased during your shopping trip. You are typically considered an independent contractor—meaning, you are responsible for paying your own taxes at the end of the year (or quarterly if you prefer).

There are various types of mystery shops:

Video(ed) mystery shops consists of spying on your target. During these shopping events, you'll visit senior citizen homes and other places of business, wearing video equipment to record the entire mystery shopping experience. During this kind of mystery shopping, as with all other types, you must complete the assignment to the required specifications. Video shops offer a higher pay, and the required equipment typically has to be bought or rented, with you bearing the cost.

Restaurant shops typically involve visiting fast-food, family, and fine-dining establishments. During these visits, you will typically order specific food items (like appetizers, a dessert, a main entrée, etc.) and then report back on the quality of the food and service you received. You will also pay close attention to the timing of the interactions. Many companies reimburse for the cost of the food only, whereas some pay a shop fee and reimburse for the food.

Hospitality shops usually include hotels. With this kind of mystery shopping, you will probably receive a free night's stay in a hotel and perhaps a fee. You may also be asked to evaluate casinos, spas, cruises, and other high-end hospitality services. This assignment will have strict limits, and you may only complete one in a certain amount of time. In addition, these types of shops are typically reserved for experienced shoppers.

Home, apartment, and car shops are types of mystery shopping during which you may be asked to pose as a person looking for an apartment or purchasing a new home and/or to test-drive a certain model car. You will then be paid a shop fee for your time. These type of assignments typically require extensive reports so you will often have long narratives to fill out.

Additional mystery shopping tips:

- If you have an iPhone, you may want to download an app like ShopIt Time and Stealth Notes, which enables you to make recordings, take photos, and add notes during your mystery shop. To an everyday user, the app looks like you're texting someone; however, to the professional mystery shopper, it is a great way to record interactions.

- You may initially take the lower-paid shops in order to be considered for higher-paying assignments. No matter the pay, take your time and exceed expectations. Always follow directions, and be discreet when you're taking notes on your phone or recording the interaction with your video camera. These actions go a long way toward establishing you as a professional mystery shopper.

- Be prepared in advance. Read and understand shop details before you head out to the shop location. Understand what things you're evaluating and the details you must obtain. Check your batteries if you need to record the interaction and confirm you have enough available storage space on your smartphone. If you don't, and your battery dies in the middle of the assignment, you may only be paid a partial fee or no fee at all.

- Complete the assignments thoroughly and accurately. Proofread your report before you submit it and explain any discrepancies you find in the narrative. For instance, if a multiple-choice question asked, "Was the employer properly dressed?" and you answered, "No," also address this no answer in your narrative or summary. Tell why you marked your answer as no by explaining that they were wearing jeans, didn't have on the correct uniform, or anything that may prove your no response.

- Only accept assignments that you know you will to complete on time. If you don't think you can complete it, contact your scheduler right away and ask for an extension. In most instances, they will grant one. If you flake out on an assignment, you will receive a bad citation, and it will ultimately reflect on your opportunities for securing future shop work.

- Pay close attention to all interactions so that you can provide your client with a comprehensive report. If the shop details state that you can't bring children along, then don't bring them. In some instances, the establishment will tape the interaction, and they'll go back to review the tape and see that you didn't follow instructions.

- If possible, wait until the middle to the end of the month to accept assignments so that you can receive bonuses from schedulers. Oftentimes schedulers offer these bonuses to entice shoppers to take shops—usually done toward the end of the month.

- If you're ever asked to expand on a report or to make corrections, don't take it personally. Editors at some mystery shopping companies can be real sticklers for details, so just give them the information required within twelve hours or less to avoid any issues.

Doing all these things will help you gain a solid reputation as a mystery shopper and will open up new assignments for you.

Below we will discuss some mystery shopping companies that may hire you to complete assignments.

Mystery Shopping Company #1 – Secret Shopper

Secret Shopper has been in business for over twenty-five years. They have assisted with assignments for banks, restaurants, health care institutions, museums, galleries, retail and grocery stores, gyms, salons, hotels and resorts, casinos, real estate, and automobiles. Secret

Shopper strives to deliver excellence to their clients.

Requirements to be a Secret Shopper:

- No prior experience is required
- Must be reliable, dependable
- Must be detailed-oriented
- Must have exceptional written communication skills
- Must have access to a computer
- Must have access to a digital camera or scanner
- Must meet deadlines
- Must be at least eighteen years old

There is no charge to be a Secret Shopper; however; some assignments may require you to make a purchase during your assignment. These purchases are reimbursed or calculated into the payment for the assignment. Each assignment has different instructions and payments. The normal pay per assignment is between $12–$25. Checks are sent out on the twentieth of each month for assignments completed the month before. The checks are only valid for ninety days and should be deposited or cashed as soon as possible.

Where to Sign Up: https://www.secretshopper.com/

Mystery Shopping Company #2 – IntelliShop

IntelliShop is located in Perrysburg, Ohio. They serve a number of industries, such as automotive, banking, clothing, real estate, media, advertising, food service, and museums.

To increase your shopper rating, be sure to:

- Follow guidelines closely.

- Finish assignments on time.
- Write thorough mystery shopping reports.

They rate your reports on a numeric system, ten being the best and one being the worst. Their system is tough because they hold very high standards for their mystery shoppers. Assignments are typically edited and rated by senior-level editors.

Payments will be sent through PayPal in about thirty days from the last day of the month of your completed assignments. It could take an additional five days for the money to post to PayPal. They do not issue checks as payment. There is no indication on the amount of pay for each assignment.

Where to Sign Up: http://www.intelli-shop.com/

Mystery Shopping Company #3 – BestMark

BestMark is partnered with companies in various industries. They take pride in their quality standards and even turn away millions of dollars' worth of business to keep the quality of their business in high standing.

They seek those who have a keen eye, and are responsible and conscientious about their commitments. You must also meet deadlines and follow detailed instructions.

Mystery Shopping Requirements

- Must be at least nineteen years old
- Must have reliable transportation
- Must possess excellent written communication skills
- Must be focused
- Must have full access to the Internet
- No previous experience is required

Complete their online application and then you will be contacted when assignments become available in your area. Compensation for an assignment can vary from cash payments, reimbursements, or a combination of the two. The payment will be thoroughly discussed in the details of the assignment before you decide to take it. Payment for assignments usually takes three to four weeks after completion. Checks will be mailed to you. They do not make payments through PayPal.

Where to Sign Up: http://www.bestmark.com/

Mystery Shopping Company #4 – Market Force

Market Force was founded in 2005 and has a global presence in the United States, Canada, France, Germany, and the United Kingdom. They have over 350 clients and complete over one hundred thousand mystery shops a month.

Sign up for free to become a mystery shopper with Market Force. You will be paid to visit local stores or brands as a regular shopper and then report back with your findings. You can even use their mobile app, Eyes:On, to shop on the go. The app is available for iPhone, iPad, and Android. In return, you will receive a shopper payment or reimbursement for meals or free purchases. There is no mention of how they pay or the amount they pay per assignment.

Where to Sign Up: https://www.marketforce.com/

Mystery Shopping Company #5 – Coyle Hospitality Group

Coyle Hospitality Group, founded in 1996, is a market leader in designing and implementing mystery shopping. Their areas of expertise include hotels, spas, restaurants, cruises, resorts, and time-shares. They have done over 65,000 evaluations since 1996.

Businesses hire companies such as this one to conduct research about their businesses. Mystery shoppers pose as customers and engage in normal customer activities in order to evaluate the company.

Requirements:

- Cell phone
- Reliable transportation
- Digital camera
- Computer
- Internet connection
- Timepiece
- Access to a fax machine
- PayPal account
- Credit/debit card that can receive several hundred dollars
- Stopwatch
- Microsoft Office software
- Scanner

Once you register, you will have access to over four hundred known companies just in North America. This does not count the other geographic areas that the company covers. Most companies will pay between $5–$15, plus reimbursements. Some shop opportunities can pay $100 or more, and they have many hotel shops where you'll receive a shop fee and reimbursement for one night at an exclusive hotel property. They also have numerous high-end restaurant shops that pay $20 plus reimbursement of the meal. In some instances, you can evaluate the same location more than once, assuming that you've met the "wait requirement."

Where to Sign Up: http://www.coylehospitality.com/mystery-shopping-services/

Mystery Shopping Company #6 – Ellis Partners Management Solutions

Ellis Partners Management Solutions was established in 1984 and is one of the most respected executive-level management and marketing consulting services, centering around apartment mystery shopping and resident surveys.

To get started as an apartment mystery shopper, fill out the online application. Review and complete the independent contractor agreement. Choose which contract opportunities you want to explore. Complete your assignment in a timely manner. You may be asked to purchase a product, and you will pose as a real customer. You will be paid once a month through direct deposit. Most of the assignments pay $30–$40 each; however, it could take up to two to three hours to complete the site evaluation. These evaluations are quite comprehensive, so be as thorough as possible when filling out your shop report, or it may be rejected.

Where to Sign Up: http://epmsonline.com/

33. Make Money as a Movie Trailer Checker

Do you enjoy watching movie trailers? Do you like going to the movies? Are you detail-oriented and organized, and do you enjoy collecting data? If you answered yes to these questions, you will probably enjoy working as a movie trailer checker. In this position, you will typically spend two to three hours—or fifteen to thirty minutes—in various theaters in order to view ads and trailers, count patrons who enter the theater, and more. You will basically act as a research consultant, gathering information that theaters and companies who sponsor ads need for market research purposes.

With "open" movie checking, you make a revealed audit so theater management is typically aware of your activities. During the process, you will collect information via questionnaires and forms (paper and online).

Some revealed audits include:

- **Theater lobby check** – During this check, you visit the theater and evaluate any promotional material in the theater or lobby and take photos of the material.

- **Trailer checks** – During this assignment, you basically watch and write down all the trailers shown on the screens (before the selected movie offering) at the assigned theater.

- **Audience reaction checks** – During a reaction evaluation, you watch and record the audience's reactions to various trailers.

- **Seat counts** – During a seat count, you count the number of patrons that attended assigned showtimes and collect box office information at the end of the movie.

- **Ad checker** – As an ad checker, you write down the name and type of ad before the trailers of assigned features. With this one, you typically arrive fifteen minutes before showtime, and you keep a record of all ads and previews shown before the movie starts.

- **Sneak preview** – During a sneak preview, you visit sneak previews to see movies not yet released. You'll then count the number of patrons; evaluate customers' reactions to trailers, ads, and movies; and evaluate picture and sound quality.

During an unrevealed audit, the managerial staff is unaware of your visit. So, in essence, you are working as a secret shopper, and you must ensure that you covertly take notes and make recordings. An example of a blind check would be to visit selected theaters to secretly count all the patrons who attended various shows.

You will work on the opening days of major productions, which is typically on Fridays, Saturdays, or Sundays. You can pick and choose your hours, the days you want to visit, the types of assignments, and the theaters that you want to visit.

What It Pays

As a movie trailer checker, you can earn anywhere from $7–$10 per hour; however, experienced checkers can earn up to $45 an hour. Some assignments pay a flat rate, and others pay hourly. Typically every assignment has a price tag, depending on the amount of hours you put in and what you are asked to check. As for the number of hours, you could work thirty to forty-five minutes or all day. Any evaluation that involves more time, advanced evaluations, and multiple locations will obviously pay more.

Requirements:

- You must be over eighteen with reliable transportation and Internet access.

- You must have a camera, plus a laptop or desktop computer with reliable scanner, fax, and Internet service.

The job is extremely entertaining and fun, but projects may be sporadic; therefore, you should sign up with a bunch of companies to ensure a steady flow of projects.

Additional tips for becoming a great mystery shopper:

- Set aside time after your assignment to make notes. You will be less likely to forget important details when completing the assignment.

- Make a mystery shop folder. Keep all your assignments in this folder so they do not get lost.

- Regularly check the job boards on whichever site you are using. Checking on a consistent basis will give you a better chance of landing an assignment.

- When reporting, provide as much detail about your assignment as possible.

- Stay ahead of deadlines.

- Have fun!

Does this sound interesting to you? The job is extremely entertaining, fun, and satiating. Here are various companies that hire individuals for movie checking positions:

Movie Trailer Checker Company #1 – VeriTES

VeriTES hires independent contractors in all fifty states, Canada, and Puerto Rico to provide mystery shopping. Some of the assignments may include cinemas, department stores, restaurants, and other specialty stores. They provide essential marketing data to corporations through the eyes and ears of their independent contractors who do the mystery shops. Assignments are usually given out for Friday evenings and throughout the day on Saturdays and Sundays. A predetermined flat fee is paid to the mystery shopper, and this will vary from assignment to assignment. You will be paid by check after the assignment is completed.

Movie Trailer Checker Company #2 – Market Force

Market Force is a mystery shopping company founded in 2005. They complete over one hundred thousand mystery shops each month and process millions of employee and customer surveys. Sign up for free as a mystery shopper with this site. You must be at least eighteen years old and have at least a high school diploma. As a mystery shopper, you will be helping local stores and restaurants better serve their customers. You can even shop on the go with their mobile app, Eyes:On, which is available for Android and Apple. You will receive a shopper payment or reimbursement for free meals and purchases after you have completed your assignment. You will be paid once a month with a check or via direct deposit for all approved assignments.

Movie Trailer Checker Company #3 – Confero

Confero is one of the leading providers for customer experience research and mystery shopping. Many of their clients are household names. Mystery shopping can be conducted in restaurants, convenience and grocery stores, drug stores, banks, medical practices, airports, theme parks, and movie theaters.

To be a mystery shopper with Confero, you must be at least twenty-one years old and have:

- An open mind
- An ability to remember and report facts and observations
- An ability to write up reports about findings
- Internet access
- Reliable transportation
- A PayPal account

To work for Confero, create an online account and complete a profile. You will be asked for your name, address, and email address, which will help match you with assignments. You will be contacted through email by a scheduler if you live or work near an assignment location. You can also access the job board and apply for assignments once you are logged into the system. The amount of money that can be made will vary from assignment to assignment. You will know how much the assignment pays before you decide to accept it. Information on the methods and timing of payments is outlined in their payment policy.

34. Make Money by Merchandising

Have you ever been to a grocery store, movie theater, or drug store and been impressed by an end-cap display or noticed a really amazing product display that inspired you to buy? If so, you've probably just witnessed clever advertising at work and seen, firsthand, how important a merchandiser is for selling products. Merchandising has been around for decades and is typically used to promote a movie, personal care, grocery or other type of item. It involves the careful arrangement of items so that customers are drawn to them.

The average newbie merchandiser makes about $11.78 per hour, which equates to $25,000 a year working full-time. However, more experienced fashion merchandisers make about $40,340 or more a year. Plus, when you combine this opportunity with mystery shopping, the income increases substantially. The amount you make will depend largely on your geographical area, tenure, and specific employers/clients. Some merchandisers work as independent contractors.

As a merchandiser, you will ensure goods are in the right store at the right time and right place, devise and revise advertising campaigns, order supplies and goods, liaise with other departments, produce sales projects, set up and take down displays, report sales projections, analyze sales data, and negotiate with suppliers.

To excel at this position, a degree is useful but not required. You must be hardworking, dedicated, creative, flexible, and people-focused. You'll need excellent time management, people management, monitoring, administrative, mathematical, organizational, and decision-making skills. Plus you should have an in-depth knowledge of computers, effective writing, sales and marketing, interpersonal relationships, critical thinking, as well as a meticulous attention to detail.

Additional Tips:
- It can be hard to fulfill a more-than-forty-hour requirement with one company, so many merchandisers work for five or

more companies to get enough hours. Oftentimes they also work as mystery shoppers to increase income opportunities. Or they mix up monthly, weekly, and occasional work with different companies to keep busy and improve their bottom line.

- Always do your due diligence research before signing up with any merchandising companies.

- If you have any physical limitations, this might not be the best opportunity for you, as you will likely be required to lift objects over fifteen pounds and will spend a lot of time on your feet.

- Keep a written schedule. It can be hard juggling all your merchandising projects. To ensure no overlaps happen, write down what you must do on a daily, weekly, and monthly basis.

- Create a stellar résumé and then list it on Retail Jobs North America (formerly NARMS) and The Retail Recruiter so that you can receive a steady influx of opportunities.

- Follow merchandising instructions carefully. For instance, if it says that you will only be paid for five hours in the store, contact headquarters to ask for approval before extending your time or you risk not being paid for the extra time.

Merchandising Opportunity #1 – CROSSMARK

CROSSMARK is a marketing services company, providing innovative marketing solutions for companies worldwide. They have offices in the United States, Mexico, New Zealand, Australia, and Canada.

They regularly offer positions for independent contractors. These are short-term assignments that range from finding products to getting their prices and details for wholesale or retail contracts.

They also have Shopper Engagement Experts positions, who go around sampling, demonstrating, or serving as brand ambassadors for products.

Payment is sent weekly, and, to get more projects, you must develop a good work performance rating with this company. This means, if you are booked for four hours, you must stay the entire time and work efficiently to complete the task. The hourly rate is minimum pay, and they have a policy of "No work, no pay," which means, if for some reason you can't work (even for a valid reason, like inclement weather), you won't get paid. However, the good news is that they always pay on time.

Where to Sign Up: http://www.crossmark.com/

Merchandising Opportunity #2 – Premium Retail

Premium Retail offers retail merchandising. Part-time merchandisers are allowed to work flexible hours with reasonable quotas. The company is employee-friendly and is known to follow the employees' preferred schedules. You are required to complete forms when given an assignment, which must be submitted to your immediate superior. The company will pay for gas mileage, and the pay rate is approximately $12 per hour. This is really a part-time job and will not compensate you enough to live comfortably on this job alone. One way to get a higher pay rate is to become an expert in a product—so much so that you get priority over other employees.

This solid company has an excellent reputation among their workers.

Where to Sign Up: http://premiumretail.com/

Merchandising Opportunity #3 – Castforce

Castforce is a group of independent retail merchandisers based in Florida. They claim to work with top brands in the country and offer thousands of retail merchandising opportunities.

To join their group, simply sign up on their website. They will ask you a lot of questions to start with, so you must be ready with your answers and willing to part with some personal information.

As an independent merchandiser, you get to pick your hours. Payout is done once a month through mailed checks, and you can accept as many jobs as you can handle. Most projects are simple and easy-to-finish. Pay is based on the specific job, but it generally pays about $15 an hour.

Where to Sign Up: http://castforce.com/

Merchandising Opportunity #4 – American Greetings

American Greetings is a household name, so it should be reassuring to anyone interested in working part-time with them. They have full-time and part-time jobs for merchandisers. The part-time merchandisers are assigned stores, which they have to visually inspect and spend time in. Part of their job is checking card stock, fixing displays, and restocking supplies. They must clock in and out whenever they visit an assigned store. Salaries and pay start at $7 an hour but go up to $15, depending on experience. You must work weekends and holidays.

Where to Sign Up:
http://corporate.americangreetings.com/careers/careerareas/PTM_jobs.html

35. Making Money as a Babysitter

Babysitting is a great way to earn extra money. No formal training is required to be a babysitter. Many websites allow you to build a profile, and then members can contact you if they feel you are a good fit for their family. Babysitters earn an average hourly wage of $9.40. However, you can establish how much to charge for your services. If you are offering babysitting services in your home, check the state laws to see if a license is required to do so. You will also be responsible for income taxes, as you will be considered an independent contractor. A local tax professional can help you with this.

Here are some considerations to take into account when establishing how much to charge:

- How much experience do you have?
- What is the cost of living in your area?
- How many children will you be babysitting at one time?
- What are the ages of the children you will be babysitting?
- Will you be responsible for taking them to activities outside the home?
- Will you be responsible for driving some of them to school and back home?
- What time of day will your services be needed?
- Do any of the children have special needs?
- Are you certified in CPR and first aid?
- Are you required to do light housekeeping when babysitting in the client's home?

All the things mentioned above will influence how much you charge for your babysitting services. Below we will discuss some of the websites where you can build a profile about the services you offer.

Babysitting Opportunity #1 – Care.com

Care.com has over 20.7 million members and covers sixteen countries. Not only can you offer babysitting services on this site but you can also offer adult and senior care, pet care, and home care. Sign up for a free account. After you have completed that process, then create a profile. This is where you will list your talents and skills, along with a photo. You can also browse jobs posted on the site. Once you find a match, apply to the job. You are paid through direct deposit.

Where to Sign Up: http://www.care.com

Babysitting Opportunity #2 – Enanny

Enanny specializes in helping families find nannies (from live-in to live-out, for permanent or temporary positions), babysitters, and infant specialists. Their goal is to help you find the right job with the right family. They offer expert advice and guidance to help you along the way. Once you have registered for a free account, you should post an in-depth profile, searchable by those seeking a caregiver for their child/children.

You will also have access to profiles for families and can get in touch with those who may be a good fit for you. Plus you'll have a personalized account which keeps track of jobs you are interested in and the families who may have contacted you for an interview. Your personal information is kept private and will never be listed on the site. You will receive daily emails with jobs that you may be interested in.

Where to Sign Up: https://www.enannysource.com/Home.aspx

Babysitting Opportunity #3 – UrbanSitter

UrbanSitter was founded by four parents as an online resource where parents can go and find babysitters. Over fifty thousand caregivers are available in over sixty cities nationwide. To begin, create a free account. After you have completed the sign-up, create your profile, including your availability and babysitting rates. Parents can then find your profile and contact you if interested in hiring you for their babysitting needs. Once you have been contacted, respond to the request and decide if it is a good fit for you. After the parents make payment, it will take three full business days to process the payment to your bank account.

Remember that a family looking for a babysitter is looking for someone with the following personality traits and qualifications:

- Patient
- Loves children
- Responsible
- Flexible as to scheduling
- Sensitive
- Experienced
- Energetic
- Playful
- Trustworthy

Where to Sign Up: https://www.urbansitter.com/

36. Make Money Pet Sitting

Everybody loves their pets. They can't get enough of them and are willing to spend money to keep them happy and healthy. Based on the IBIS World study on the pet grooming-boarding industry, this business is growing at a rate of 6.6% annually and is now worth over $7 billion USD. Of this amount about $5.24 billion is spent on boarding alone. Even more interesting, an estimated eighty million homes in the United States have at least one pet. This means that the pet boarding industry has barely scratched the surface, and one of the options fast catching up with boarding is pet sitting. So if you love pets, you should definitely consider a position as a pet sitter.

What is Pet Sitting?

Pet sitting is taking care of the dog, cat, or any other pets, typically in their familiar environment—their home and surrounding community. Instead of taking the pet to a professional boarding facility, pet owners are now opting to have someone honest, friendly, and well-trained with animals to care for their pets in their own homes.

This type of business is quite steady and began in the 1970s when families started earning double incomes to maintain their lifestyles. Rather than bring the pet to a boarding facility, they would ask someone to come and check on their pet. It is estimated that, because few pet sitters are around the country, they get to collectively post up to sixty million home visits a year.

The scope of a pet-sitting service includes the following, although not necessarily limited to these:

- Walking
- Playing
- Feeding
- Grooming

- Administering medicine or vitamins
- Cleaning the pet's area

Some clients also make special requests, such as bringing in the mail, checking the house for break-ins or damages by the pet, watering indoor plants, taking out the trash, and other similar small tasks.

The Basic Qualifications to Get Hired as a Pet Sitter

First and foremost, you must love pets. Additionally you should:

- Be willing to walk, groom, feed, play, and care for pets
- Be physically fit, plus mentally and emotionally healthy
- Be business-minded
- Be experienced in basic training on how to care for animals
- Have insurance and/or a fidelity bond
- Be available even on weekends, holidays, and for emergency situations
- Have excellent communication skills
- Be willing to work overtime if needed
- Be a member of a pet-sitting club (like Pet Sitters International) or have certification in animal care

Many people assume that pet sitting is limited to dogs and cats, but many residents and pet owners have other types of pets to care for (like birds, horses, fish, small reptiles), including smaller animals (like rats, hamsters, and guinea pigs).

How to Get Certified

Some of the organizations that offer certifications as a pet sitter are PetTech, American Red Cross, and PetCo, which all teach first aid training for animals. A curriculum should include pet health, pet care, nutrition, animal laws, animal behavior, and business development and management. Also important are the ethics in caring for other people's pets.

How Much Does a Pet Sitter Make?

Your rating as a pet sitter will depend on your skills, training, and experience. Your marketing skills and networking assets will also come into play because, the more in demand your services are, the higher your income—not because you can charge a higher rate, but because loyal clients will be willing to give you bigger tips and refer you to more clients.

However, to give you a realistic view, based on one person's personal experience as a pet sitter, she charges $15 an hour and can accept up to eight clients a day, not including weekends. This amounts to about $30,000 annually. You can make more because, based on a 2010 study, a pet sitter with 103 clients can earn up to $48,635 a year!

How to Get Started Working as a Pet Sitter

You can sign up with a number of credible companies to get started as a pet sitter. The advantage of this includes not having to raise capital to start your own business and not having to wait before you see any ROI. As a pet sitter accredited with an established business, you can slowly build your reputation, and any minimal investment you spend (getting trained, etc.) will quickly be recovered with regular sitting jobs.

Tips for Pet Sitting

- ✓ Communicate with the pet owner.

- ✓ Learn how to ascertain if the pet is trained or has special needs by asking the owner questions. If you feel you cannot handle the pet, best not to book the job. Watch out for some pet behaviors—including food aggression, antisocial tendencies, separation anxiety issues, or sickly pets—before accepting those pet-sitting jobs.

- ✓ Be clear about pick-up or drop-off times and overtime rates.

- ✓ If the pet will be staying in your home, create a designated area for the pet that the owner can view. It should include a sleeping area with some visible system for feeding and potty times.

- ✓ Be specific about why you are a pet sitter, your schedule, and experience.

- ✓ Send pictures of you with their pet if the owner agrees but make sure the photos are not selfies, and only include you and the pet.

Finally, consider signing up with at least two sites so you get more job offers. Here are some places to consider:

Pet-Sitting Company #1 – Rover

Rover is a great income opportunity because it gives you 80% of your pay from your sitting jobs. You set your own rates and are paid via PayPal.

This company started in Seattle in 2011 and is now in most states across the country. You must create a profile and be assessed before accepted on their roster. Rover needs to see if you and your home qualify as a sitter, and part of the screening process includes submitting photos. Based on what you submit—and if you qualify—you get coaching, advice, a great profile page on their site, and a welcome package well worth over $200.

Where to Sign Up: http://www.rover.com

Pet-Sitting Company #2 – Pet Sitter

Pet Sitter is one of the companies under CareGuide that offers all sorts of freelance jobs in the United States and Canada. This company is similar to many freelance websites in that it acts like a classified ad site for different kinds of jobs. Getting started is so simple. Create a profile for free and bid for jobs posted on their website. You can also post your rate and services on the site, and wait for queries to come in.

The average rate you earn on Pet Sitter is $11.25 an hour, though you must compete with other sitters for a job.

Where to Sign Up: http://petsitter.com/

Pet-Sitting Company #3 – Fetch! Pet Care

Fetch! Pet Care started in 2002 as a boarding business with a humane approach to handling animals. Over the years they branched out to pet sitting, pet walking, overnight care, and a pet taxi service. They now franchise their business and are present in many states.

To become a sitter, you must find a Fetch! Pet Care office near you, fill out their online application, and wait for a response from that local office. Usually the business owner will request a meeting to assess if you will be a good fit for them.

The requirements of Fetch! Pet Care include:

- Willingness to work flexible hours
- Previous experience with animal sitting and/or care
- Love of animals
- Willingness to attend an orientation on services

Your earnings will depend on the amount of time you are willing to give to sitting pets and your skills as a sitter. The average rate ranges from $15 to $30 per hour, but the business owner will take 50% for his operating expenses and profit, which means you make anywhere from $7.50 to $15 per job.

Where to Sign Up: https://www.fetchpetcare.com/

Pet-Sitting Company #4 – Dog Vacay

Dog Vacay is a community that offers services online. The system is simple. Create an account and start offering your services. Any booking is done through the website, and Dog Vacay gets 20% as their hosting fee. Payments are made either through check by mail or PayPal.

Accepting jobs outside of the website, even if the client responded to your ad on their site, means you forfeit any insurance coverage should anything happen to you or the pet. You also risk being blacklisted by the business, which will undoubtedly damage your reputation in the industry.

Where to Sign Up: https://dogvacay.com

Pet-Sitting Company #5 – Pet Sitters

Pet Sitters (or PSI) started in 1983 as one of the pioneers in the industry. The founder is Patti Moran, also known for writing an authoritative book on pet sitting. To work with PSI, you must become a member. A first-year membership fee is $150, which includes the application fee. For succeeding years, members pay annual dues of $140. The company does not collect any fees from jobs booked.

As a member, you get to create your own business page, have access to insurance and bonding, obtain free advice and consultation on pet-sitting services plus promotional materials, and, most important of all, gain accreditation as a member of the most respected professional pet-sitting organization in the world.

Where to Sign Up: https://www.petsit.com/

37. Make Money with Clinical Trials

Feel like being a guinea pig for the sake of research and to make some extra cash? Clinical trials, or treatment research, are medical research studies that have graduated from initial testing and are now ready for human testing. Many clinical trials are ongoing at any given time, and not all of them require you to ingest a new drug or formula. Some trials are for new vitamins, new gadgets, or new lifestyle therapies. Most of them pay fairly, and others pay handsomely.

Some trials require you to check in as an inpatient while others treat you as outpatients. Clinical trials consist of four phases, according to the Food and Drug Administration (FDA). The first phase is a small group trial, followed by a larger group (Phases 2 and 3). The last phase is done after the FDA approves the product and is on the market—like a post-marketing study.

Under the FDA guidelines, anyone who participates in a clinical trial must be protected. This means, if you decide you want to make money on the side by participating in a clinical trial, these are your rights:

- You are told what the trial is for and agree in writing with regard to the risks, benefits, and side effects.

- You must be informed of the scope of the trial: the actual testing and follow-up meetings.

- You cannot be coerced into participating unless you have a life-threatening situation, confirmed by an independent doctor.

- You must be an adult or get parental consent.

- The trial is conducted by a group registered with the FDA and the ClinicalTrials.org.

Additional Tips for Successful Clinical Trial Participation

- ✓ Make sure the terms of the trial are clear and in writing. Plus request a copy that you can take home with you.

- ✓ Don't give up if you were not selected the first time.

- ✓ Confirm that the company is duly recognized by the national health agencies, especially the FDA and the US Department of Health and Human Services. This ensures that these clinical trial companies have the appropriate license to conduct such trials.

Finally ask as many questions as needed to avoid any confusion or to address any concerns you may have but do this before you agree to participate in the trial.

Some of the companies accepting participants for clinical trials are:

Clinical Trial Site #1 – Centerwatch

Centerwatch was launched as a business in 1994 in Boston. They offer clinical trial information and research to individuals and groups alike. They also freely dispense data about clinical trials so, even if you don't participate in their trials, you can learn a lot about the business by visiting their website.

They have several trials ongoing at any given time, and, to participate, you must be screened to find out if you are eligible. Unfortunately they do not pay their participants any money but offer benefits, like inside information on new products and the knowledge that you are contributing to medical research.

Where to Sign Up: http://www.centerwatch.com/

Clinical Trial Site #2 – Covance

Covance (now owned by LabCorp, which bought Covance in 2014) is a research group based in New Jersey and present in sixty countries—one of the largest companies specific to this industry with revenues reaching over $2 billion USD.

Covance conducts more than one hundred clinical trials a year, and all it takes to get started is one phone call to 1-866-429-3700. They pay thousands of dollars to participants of their clinical studies. A quick view of what they have includes trials for healthy adults (aged eighteen to forty-five) paying up to $3,300 or for healthy women (aged eighteen to forty-five) with compensation of $2,000. Their screening includes your location and demographics (age, gender, health status). The studies can take anywhere from two days to several months. Other studies pay much more, but the screening is more specific, such as having a particular medical condition or disease.

Payment is done by check or direct deposit. You can do more than one trial, but you must wait at least one month before taking the next trial.

Where to Sign Up: https://www.covanceclinicaltrials.com/

Clinical Trial Site #3 – Elite Research Institute

Elite Research Institute conducts clinical trials to study ADHD, depression, anxiety, low back pain, hypertension, insomnia, asthma, arthritis, and many other conditions. All interested participants must go through a screening process. Qualified participants will get paid for their time and travel. They also get free medicines, free office visits, and free laboratory workups.

The compensation depends on the length and scope of the study. To become a participant, simply go their website and subscribe. Once you have a profile, you can access possible jobs and get paid up to hundreds of dollars by check after the study.

Where to Sign Up: http://www.eliteresearchinst.com/

Clinical Trial Site #4 – ACMR (Atlanta Center for Medical Research)

This group seeks volunteers willing to be paid for their time to participate in their clinical trials. They do have strict criteria, depending on the type of study to be done. For instance, a recent trial required healthy individuals yet unable to conceive. However, they must not be smokers, plus agree to stop drinking caffeine and alcohol, and avoid grapefruit for the duration of the ten-day study. The participants were paid $50 to be screened and $200 a day for ten days plus $75 for every follow-up visit. Their take-home total was around $2,400.

To sign up with the company, you must complete an online form, then wait for them to contact you.

Where to Sign Up: https://www.acmr.org/

Clinical Trial Site #5 – Spaulding Clinical

Spaulding Clinical is located in Milwaukee, so most—if not all—of their trials are done on their campus in that area. To be considered for their trials, you must sign up with them on their website. Periodically you will get SMS messages, informing you of a new study.

Many of their studies require you to participate as an inpatient for several days. When you subscribe, you get screened initially. Then, when a study is launched, your profile is viewed and screened more diligently. If you qualify, you get paid over $1,000 (depending on the length of stay), plus have free use of all amenities on campus, including accommodations and meals.

They have a toll free number you can call for more information at 1-800-597-4507.

Where to Sign Up: http://www.spauldingclinical.com/

38. Make Money as a Mock Juror

Although most people abhor mandatory jury duty, working as a paid mock juror can actually be a fun, exciting, and rewarding experience. In fact, the American Bar Association (ABA) encourages attorneys, law students, and other legal professionals to engage in mock trials as a "learning experience." To demonstrate their commitment to these trials, the ABA features several guides on mock trial preparation on their site.

During a mock trial, the participants listen to the attorneys' arguments, how the issues are framed, and how the case law is presented, and then make a decision about the case's outcome. During the mock jury, the attorneys ask comprehensive and detailed questions, and then follow up with the mock jurors to determine why they deliberated the way they did. During a contested mock trial, attorneys are allowed to further deliberate their cases in an effort to change the jurors' minds. This process enables attorneys to practice their litigation skills and strengthen any holes in their cases before taking their real case to court.

With this in mind, it's no wonder that attorneys and clients hire the services of mock jurors to plot out and enhance their legal cases before trials. As a mock juror, you'll be paid to participate in mock trials just like jurors in a real court case. The average pay of a real juror, federal or state, is about $45 a day—with food, accommodations, and transportation paid for by the government. As a mock juror, you get paid by private clients of attorneys. The fees can range from $5 to $400 a day or more, depending on the client and the complexity of the case.

To be a part of a mock jury, you must register with any one of the companies offering this income opportunity. However, be advised that, if a mock juror is required to be present in the mock trial, your geographical location could hinder your inclusion. That is, if they're only looking for people in Arkansas, then you must legally reside in Arkansas to participate. To open yourself to more opportunities, you can also work as an online mock juror; however, the competition for these spots is higher, and the pay is typically lower.

Here are some of the companies offering this unique way to earn a little extra cash:

Mock Jury Company #1 – Probe Market Research

Probe Market Research is primarily a research group based in New York that offers focus-group surveys. However, they also have mock trials, so signing up with this website offers you two income opportunities: get paid to be part of a focus group or get paid to be a mock juror.

One issue with this company is that they try to avoid using the same people again and again, so you may not always be called to participate—even if you qualify based on your demographics and location.

The company pays $50 to $400, and interviews are done online or by phone. The company pays in cash, and you must pick it up from their office.

Where to Sign Up: http://www.probemarket.com/

Mock Jury Company #2 – Resolution Research

Resolution Research comes highly recommended by media, including a special mention in an article published by *Woman's World*. This company hires more for focus groups but also has the occasional in-person mock jury—meaning, you must come in to participate and to get paid as a mock juror. The venue is usually a conference room paid for by the requesting client. Drinks and a snack are provided.

To participate as a mock juror, you must check the company website daily, although they sometimes post ads on Craigslist, in local newspapers, and on their Facebook account. Once you are preselected, another screening process is had via a questionnaire. Your answers will determine if you are to be included in the mock jury or not.

The basic criteria to be included as a mock juror are:

- Must be at least eighteen years old and a US citizen
- No prior or current convictions as a felon
- Must be able to read and write in English
- A willingness to sign a nondisclosure agreement

If you want to be part of their list for surveys, you can sign up for free at their website. The pay is anywhere from $5 (for surveys) to $400 (for mock jury duty), paid to participants in cash and to be collected from them. You can also earn through their referral system and get $0.50 for every ten referrals. If you refer at least five people, you automatically get included in their periodic draws for $100, $250, and $1,000.

Where to Sign Up: http://resolutionresearch.com/

Mock Jury Company #3 – First Court

First Court markets their services as a "private court system," which is another way of saying "mock trials." They pride themselves in paying their jurors well, along with making it easy for anyone to become a juror.

It starts by signing up with your email address and then answering some simple questions before you are contacted for a brief interview. When you have been selected for a mock trial, you will be contacted by phone or email. Their mock trials are held across the country, and each mock trial needs twenty mock jurors.

Some trials take one day, while others may take a few days. The sessions are held over a private online channel. The first deliberation takes about two to three hours, and then the group is whittled down to six for a second deliberation. Those selected to continue on for the second deliberation receive additional pay but must come in for a face-to-face meeting.

Jurors in the first online deliberation get paid at least $75, but this can increase to $125. Payments are made thru PayPal or check within seven days of the mock trial. Those selected to participate in the second deliberation get paid an additional $175 in cash immediately after the session. These six also get free meals and drinks.

Their most rigid requirement is a nondisclosure contract that must be signed prior to any session to protect the privacy of their clients.

Where to Sign Up: http://firstcourt.com/

Mock Jury Company #4 – Online Verdict

This online mock jury website was the brainchild of a group of trial consultants. They allow lawyers to post mock cases for which their members are chosen a mock jurors. To become a member, you must set up your account, which takes a few minutes. Case questions require a minimum of twenty minutes to answer but can extend to sixty minutes or more. Depending on the length of the questions to be answered, a mock juror gets paid anywhere from $20 to $60 per case. Payment is done by check once a month by mail.

With this online opportunity, you are chosen based on the client's specific requirements. In addition, you can only be selected by clients in your county of residence unless a national survey opens up.

The requirements to be on this website's roster are:

- At least eighteen years old
- US citizenship
- Agreeing to the terms and conditions of the client
- Signing up and providing specific personal details, like mailing address, age, marital status, gender, email address, and phone number, among other data

Where to Sign Up: https://www.onlineverdict.com/

Mock Jury Company #5 – Trial Juries

Trial Juries offers an online income opportunity to be a mock juror and selects their jurors based on zip code. To start the process, sign up on their website and answer a few questions. You must also comply with the standard requirements:

- At least eighteen years old
- US citizenship
- No felony conviction

The compensation of a mock juror is $30 per case, and payment is made using PayPal a few days after you complete the job. Although there are no guarantees you will be selected, there are no limits to the number of times you can be called on to participate.

Where to Sign Up:
https://www.tlextranet.com/trialjuries/signup.html

Mock Jury Company #6 – eJury

The website eJury, started by trial attorney Christopher Bagby of the Bagby Law Firm in Texas, has been around since 1999. They offer online mock jury duty, which brings down the cost for their clients and has been instrumental in making eJury one of the top names in mock jury services.

Mock jurors are paid $5 to $10 per verdict using PayPal. To be selected for mock jury duty, you must fit the criteria of the client and be from the area where the real case will eventually be heard.

The requirements to join are:

- At least eighteen years old and US citizenship
- A clean record—no felonies, misdemeanors, etc.
- Ability to read and write English

- Must not be an active lawyer or member of the legal community (legal assistant, paralegal, judge)

- Must not be working with a law firm or lawyer

- Must not be related to a lawyer

- Must not be related to or working for an insurance provider

Where to Sign Up: http://www.ejury.com/

Mock Jury Company #7 – Jury Workshop

Jury Workshop is operated by Litigations Solutions LLC in East Hartford, Connecticut. As a mock juror, you get paid $25 through PayPal. However, you must be among the first sixteen to respond to get in. The company also has paid opinion polls, although payments are in the form of points. Paid opinion polls will require to you to follow a case and voice your opinions about same. For this, you get ten points. The amount of points are evaluated, and, if you're one of the top three participants with the most points, you'll receive a $100 gift card.

The requirements to join either the mock jury or the poll-taking are as follows:

- At least eighteen years old

- US residency

- Proof of county of residence for at least six months prior to taking a mock case

- No felony record

Where to Sign Up:
http://litigationsolutions.net/juryworkshop.html

39. Make Money as a Weight Loss Coach

Although a lot of people are overweight, most have a hard time losing the extra pounds. Last year the Center for Disease Control and Prevention (CDC) released critical data stating that one-third of the adult population is overweight. Researchers also claim that individual spending on weight reduction and control has ballooned to over $147 billion, and people who have weight problems spend over $1,400 more on medical costs than those without weight issues—or about $800 per person on weight loss alone. These people really want to lose the weight and are willing to pay for assistance.

As a weight loss coach, you can help these people with their weight problems and help them avoid "rebound dieting." With your knowledge of nutrition and exercise, you can help them stop this vicious and frustrating dieting cycle. Dr. Gary Foster of the University of Pennsylvania estimates that almost 65% of those who diet will end up reverting to their old eating habits within three years, while those who lose weight quickly from a crash diet program suffer from medical issues, and only 5% will keep the weight off.

The good news is that there is help. Various companies offer weight loss services, individual and group counseling, BMI monitoring, exercise and menu planning, and other aspects related to weight loss management, such as the sale of food supplements. These companies have a roster of experts preparing the necessary plans and programs that you as a weight loss coach will be using. The demand is so high for help in the weight reduction industry, you will be inundated with clients and income opportunities.

What to Expect

Your job as a weight loss coach includes but is not limited to:

- Providing support.

- Planning diet plans and meals.

- Offering supplements and different kinds of weight loss programs, including home delivery services and meal replacements.

- Understanding the different diet plans according to weight scale, gender, age [more men (73%) are overweight than women (63%), but more women seek weight loss solutions].

You must also deal with other weight reduction plans, like surgery, fad diets, and self-diet strategies. Also a ton of competition exists within the industry itself, and there are even more issues to do with scams and fraudulent claims.

However, what is going for you is the fact that people want a plan. They are tired of their weight problems. They need coaching and are open to this idea.

What It Pays

As a weight loss coach, you can expect to earn around $19.82/hour, which is equivalent to a little over $45,000 annually. The exact amount would depend on your location, level of education, employer, and skills as a coach. It also helps if you have certifications or credentials in the field of nutrition, physical fitness, counseling, and the like. Most weight loss coaches are women, and the job satisfaction ratings are impressively high because of the medical benefits, the emotional satisfaction of having helped someone, and the monetary compensation.

Potential Employers

A few of the businesses where you can apply to be a weight loss coach are:

Weight Watch Company #1 – Weight Watchers

Weight Watchers has several positions open for those interested in helping others reach their ideal weight. This company does not discriminate against anyone based on their age, race, gender, religion, or any other significant demographic data. The earnings will depend on the position, although it ranges from $13,000 all the way to $25,000. Their pay rate for weight loss coaches starts at $8/hour and can increase to $15/hour. Experienced coaches get paid up to $55,000/year with a high hourly rate of $25. Also positions as contractors/facilitators pay as much as $99/hour.

Where to Sign Up: https://www.weightwatchers.com/job/

Weight Watch Company #2 – Rise

Rise is a 24/7 weight management app solution program with guaranteed success. They assign one coach to every member. As a coach, you have the following responsibilities:

- Provide action plans for the week.

- Offer ideas for alternative meals and snacks.

- Choose the restaurants and other establishments your client should patronize to help keep the weight off.

- Answer whatever weight-related questions your client is confused about, especially with regard to nutrition and diet.

The rate they pay their coaches is about 50% or 60% of the sales. Based on their packages that start at $10/week for a trimonthly subscription and increase to $15/week for a weekly subscription, you can already compute your income. With one client, you get paid about $15 for a trimonthly client.

Where to Sign Up: https://www.rise.us/

Weight Watch Company #3 – Retrofit

Retrofit will require you to be available for one-on-one videoconferencing with the member assigned to you. As an Expert Wellness Coach, you will also be active in feeding information to the member through the member's personal dashboard.

Your responsibilities include:

- Educating your client on the Retrofit way.
- Monitoring your client and giving your client information on diet, nutrition, and exercise.
- Keeping track of your client's progress.
- Answering any queries within twelve hours.

The criteria to be accepted as one of their Expert Wellness Coaches includes:

- A Master's Degree in Nutrition or similar areas
- Being a Registered Dietitian
- Three years' minimum coaching experience
- Excellent communications skills and memory

Their coaches get compensation ranging from $20–$50/hour, and some coaches get commissions on sales.

Where to Sign Up: https://www.retrofitme.com/careers/

Weight Watch Company #4 – Nutrisystem

This weight loss program is based on portion-controlled eating combined with regular exercise. Their program promises weight loss of one to two pounds a week. As a counselor, the minimum rate is $15/hour, and this can lead to $42,590 annually, plus bonuses.

Your advantage as a counselor for Nutrisystem is the top-notch reputation of the company. Currently it is ranked ninth by experts among the easiest diet plans to follow. You are required to work on weekends and holidays, and there is usually a hiring spree toward the end of the year.

Where to Sign Up:
http://www.nutrisystem.com/jsp/careers/index.jsp

40. Make It Happen!

Do you feel as if you have more than enough to choose from? I certainly hope so. There should be more than enough active income streams to explore in order to keep your money flowing. If not, I've got you covered with an additional financial resource.

I've also written a book entitled *Passive Income Streams: How to Create and Profit from Passive Income Even if You Are Cash-Strapped and a Little Bit Lazy (But Motivated)!* This book teaches you how to make passive income even when you're not working traditional hours.

The beauty of passive income is that you can combine it with your active income streams to make even more money. I do this and recommend that you do this as well. However, you can't just sit idly by and expect money to fall in your lap. You've got to go out there and make it happen.

Take it from me, your income possibilities are endless. By having the right mind-set, working the plan, and using a bit of creativity, you can meet your financial goals. Your future is up to you and whether you have the drive and determination to follow through. Make a commitment to yourself and your financial future to explore these income possibilities. You won't regret it!

I know it is possible because I've done it. If you have the will, you can find a way to do it too. Just take one step, then another, and soon you'll have enough money to cover that $500 emergency, whether it be a medical challenge, a family trip, an unforeseen job loss, or whatever else you need.

And then you may realize even bigger earnings are possible.

Now make it happen!

Bonus

Resources for Active-Income Seekers

Work-at-Home Websites

Side Hustle Nation

Nick Loper guides you through his blog so that you can have your own financial freedom. He will teach you ways to pay off debt, earn more money, use your free time more productively, learn new skills, and escape the rat race. You can join his email list called Nation to get his free report on the Five Fastest Ways to Earn More Money.

Real Ways to Earn Money Online

The primary purpose of this blog is to provide work-from-home information which you can take action on today. You will find on this blog a list of legitimate work-from-home job leads, a work-from-home directory, and hundreds of detailed reviews of various work-from-home companies.

WAHM

This website and forum states that it is one of the best resources for moms (and dads) who want to work from home. They list legitimate work-at-home opportunities from forum members and provide insider information for those seeking legitimate work-at-home opportunities. The good news is that these opportunities are updated on a daily basis, so check back often!

Workplace Like Home

This website is a community-based blog and online forum that provides quality information about working at home. Individuals can peruse articles, search business opportunities, and discuss job openings with various work-at-home companies. On this site, you may find positions within telecommuting, sales, transcription, administrative, writing, web design, and other sectors. As this site is updated daily, it's a great one to bookmark and check often.

The Suitcase Entrepreneur

Natalie offers free videos on her site, showing you five steps to getting more free time, plus the common mistakes that cost you time and money. She also does a podcast every week where she interviews guests who talk about their life and business.

The Work-at-Home Wife

This blog has many links to work-at-home jobs, along with blogging advice and how to find jobs online. It offers a seven-day Work From Home series when you sign up for the newsletter. Also job leads are updated frequently with legitimate work-at-home jobs.

The Work-at-Home Woman

This blog was created by a mom who was looking to make extra money online after her baby was born. After searching through various websites and sifting through scams, she decided to write her own work-at-home resource blog for women. You can find leads to just about any type of job, such as direct sales, blogging for money, event planning, medical transcription, and tons of others.

Dream Home-Based Work

This blog provides and advertises legitimate ways to earn extra money, started by Lashay Hudson, a full-time blogger and stay-at-home mother. Her inspiration to start the blog was when she found herself caught in moneymaking scams and pyramid schemes. She wanted a place where people could find real work minus the scams. If you are looking to have a balanced lifestyle, keep up with this blog. New work-at-home opportunities are posted often, giving you a chance to apply for opportunities you may not have known existed.

Home-Based Mommie

This website/blog has several functions and was designed to be almost a one-stop shop for work-at-home job seekers. This website provides tips for your interviews to increase your chances of receiving a job offer. It also offers work-at-home courses, designed to help you on your way to becoming a full-time home-based employee. The website also includes a handy job search tool, books, videos, and information on how to start your own blog.

Entrepreneurship

Chris Gillebeau/The Art of Nonconformity

This website focuses on three core areas: life, work, and travel. Chris uses no outside advertising, and you can follow along using his RSS. He writes about entrepreneurship and other kinds of unconventional work. Also he writes about life planning and personal development, as well as his travels and journeys.

Tropical MBA

Dan and Ian share strategies that they used to build their business. They do a weekly podcast that covers varying topics. When subscribing, you get weekly emails that includes content about Tropical MBA news and the location independent scene.

US News Money

This blog provides nine different websites where you can earn extra money online. All the websites offer great opportunities for anyone looking to earn money from home. The contributor of this website is Trent Hamm, who created the site The Simple Dollar, which helps people become more financially savvy.

Freelancing and Internet Marketing

Warrior Forum

This Internet marketing forum is considered one of the most renowned and established of those on the Net. It includes pertinent forum posts, articles, short reports, and information about Internet marketing, advertising, making money online, buying and flipping websites, search engine placement, optimization, and much more. It is perfect for experienced and newbie marketers. Another benefit of membership is that you can offer Warrior Special Offers (WSOs) to other members of the forum who might need your specialized services.

Digital Forum

This search engine optimization and Internet marketing forum is also very well-known. It includes industry news, articles, and more for you to learn about search engine optimization, online marketing, freelancing, and so on. On Digital Forum, they also have a marketplace, where you can sell domain names, websites, graphic design/article writing, and other services. This forum also provides tools, like analytic charts, search engine position trackers, URL encoders, and more.

Upwork

Upwork is a freelance marketplace where employers and service providers interact to get projects done. They list all types of writing, translation, graphic design, and administrative projects. In addition to their job-matching services, they offer a host of great articles on freelancing and outsourcing. They also offer many resources to help freelancers succeed.

Sites about Writing as an Active Income Source

ProBlogger

If you have a love of writing and want to add another income stream, ProBlogger is a great resource. ProBlogger is a blog itself, set up to help aspiring bloggers produce their best work. This blog was started by author and speaker Darren Rowse, who is a professional blogger himself. Receive advice via website, subscription, and podcast, all designed to teach you the ins and outs of using blogging to earn extra cash.

Be a Freelance Blogger

Sophie Lizard gives practical advice on her website on how to build a portfolio and get your work out there for everyone to see. She also has guest bloggers who provide advice on how to get started. She offers three training and coaching courses: *Get Started in 28 Days*, *Get Fantastic Clients*, and *One-to-One Mentoring*.

The Write Life

On this site, you will learn how to be a freelance writer, how to go about marketing your written material, and how to be a self-publisher and blogger. Many great articles discuss things like writer's block and freelance writing clients. You can also join the community to receive free writing tips through email.

Location180

This site is about helping you build a business that you can run from anywhere and about living a life worth writing about. It offers a free email course called Six Steps to Location Independence, as well as a step-by-step guide to starting a blog.

Sites and Forums on How to Become a Photographer

The Photo Forum

The Photo Forum has 199,672 members and over 3,394,465 posts, and is perfect for the experienced or newbie photographer. It features photo contests, camera and photography equipment reviews, discussions about photography basics plus advanced photography techniques, a professional and aspiring photographer gallery, alternative techniques, HDR discussions, and much more.

Photography Talk

The Photography Talk forum is a great place for photographers to share information online. It was founded in 2010. Although it isn't aesthetically pleasing, it is chock-full of information. At this site, you'll find various learning tools, including articles, like "The Ultimate Guide to Buying Used Lenses," plus feel free to search his Learn tab and the Explore tab too for various photography tips. As for communicating with other photographers, you can certainly do your share of communicating here. You'll find photographer discussions, interviews, and even specific information on camera equipment by brand, like Nikon and Canon.

The Australian Photography Forum

This well-established international forum has over 20,159 members. Newbie and experienced photographers will find a great deal of interesting and educational discussions on this forum. There is also information about competitions and tips for beginners, plus about cell phone, macro, still-life, nature, and outdoor photography, along with so much more. It's definitely a site to check out.

Amateur Photographer

This forum has over 47,614 members and specifically caters to new photographers. It features courses, unbiased reviews to help photographers choose the perfect camera and equipment, expert photography tips, and much more. Currently posts total over 1,350,246—with an impressive gallery of 867 albums.

ClubSNAP Photography Forum

This forum features over 188,000 members. It includes an extensive gallery for photography lovers and also features categories like Travel Photography, Newbies' Corner, Food Photography, User Group Discussions, Equipment Discussions, Alternative Photography, and more. There is even an FAQ section as well.

Photoforum

This forum has over 41,622 members and 76,872 threads. It features photography categories like food, rural, panoramas and 3-D, macro, etc. You'll also find discussions about photography basics, photo critiques, people and HDR photography, and more.

Mystery Shopping Tools and Resources

JobSlinger

This is an excellent resource website that pulls all the most important job boards into one convenient place. Consider this to be your central location for mystery shopping. By opting in, you will also receive notifications to your phone, including the latest information regarding available mystery shops. JobSlinger also has an extensive knowledge base so check out its Learning Center. To subscribe for these services, fill out the information on the website to create a new account.

Mystery Shop Forum

This is a helpful forum filled with posts concerning different aspects of mystery shopping and questions that shoppers may have. Available mystery shopping assignments are regularly posted to the job board located in the forum. If you would like to engage in general chat, shoppers can meet up with others who can help guide and navigate their experience.

MS Job Board

This is a very unique site in that it lists mystery shopping assignments in real time. They have taken into consideration that many scams are on the Internet. This service screens new companies to ensure that they can be trusted to offer mystery shopping jobs to the public. The site only lists opportunities from companies they have experience with. After you register for an account, several videos are available to help you use the website and become more familiar with the service.

Shadow Shopper

This is a mystery shopping service that offers a way to hunt for available mystery jobs. When you sign up for free, you can receive email notifications of available mystery shopping assignments. You will also gain access to general education and apply for available jobs. You have the potential to unlock more opportunities later on down the line. Before you sign up, you can check to find out how many mystery shopping jobs are in your area by entering your zip code.

Job Board Opportunities

Flexjobs

This job board is an excellent source of legitimate, prescreened work-at-home opportunities. It is open to employers as well as employees. Although Flexjobs is a paid service, if you are serious about working from home, many freelancers have reported that it is well worth the investment. Serious companies looking for workers in customer service, social media management, and other remote positions are abundant on the website, and you have a great chance to find something to fit your lifestyle and your schedule.

We Work Remotely

This particular job board website is unique in that it specializes in remote opportunities not bound by any geographical area. Types of jobs are listed by category so that you can browse according to your particular interests. Some employers take creative methods in the job description to communicate the type of person who would work best within the company and for the positions offered. We Work Remotely offers an array of moneymaking opportunities and remote work options.

Rat Race Rebellion

The operators of this website take time out to prescreen the work-at-home opportunities provided to readers. Income opportunities can come from easy gigs, seasonal work, work at your leisure, independent contractor opportunities, part-time jobs, and full-time jobs. The blog posts are visually arranged, somewhat similar to Pinterest, so that you can view several opportunities across the homepage. Rat Race Rebellion always stays current with those companies taking on new hires, and has become a trusted resource for employers and potential employees. If you are in the job market and need to work from home, this will be a great resource in your arsenal of go-to websites.

Finance

The Penny Hoarder

This established financial site provides a list of different ideas which are real and for which you will get paid, because all sites have been worked by the site owners before. They guarantee some in there that you've never heard of before now.

Budgets Are Sexy

J. Money created this blog to help people stop and pay attention to their money. He offers free budget templates to get you started on making your budget and getting the most from your money. There are also money experiments, early retirement plans, sixty-plus side hustles, and a millionaires' club.

The Simple Dollar

This site was started to help people who wanted to improve their spending habits and to get out of debt. It was created to help them become financially secure. This site provides advice on stretching your money and making it grow with work-at-home opportunities.

Other Really Cool Sites to Check Out

Single Mom's Income - This website chronicles a single mother named Alexa and her journey to making it big. She learned from her past financial mistakes and, by trial and error, created income for herself on a consistent basis. She has been successful in generating about $5,000 per month. The website offers valuable resources and money management advice. Of course the website would not be complete without providing a section dedicated to making extra income. She has also thrown in information concerning business ideas that may help push you into the right direction in your search for the perfect fit for you.

Smart Passive Income – This website belongs to a guy named Pat who has dedicated himself as the test dummy for all things in the realm of passive income and online businesses. Through his experiments, you learn what to do and what not to do. Ultimately you can build your own business to bring in passive income for yourself and your family. A variety of topics are covered through the website, and a list of trusted services has also been provided to the public. If you are serious about becoming an Internet entrepreneur, feel free to check out the information on this website.

About the Author

Kristi Patrice Carter is a wife, mother, author, and serial entrepreneur who loves making active and passive income and helping others do the same. Carter's lifelong goal is to positively impact people's lives, one self-help book at a time.

A force to be reckoned with, Carter earned a Bachelor of Arts in English from the University of Illinois and a Juris Doctorate from Chicago-Kent College of Law and has over seventeen years of experience in the writing industry. She is the author of:

- *Passive Income Streams: How to Create and Profit from Passive Income Even If You're Cash-Strapped and a Little Bit Lazy (But Motivated)!*

- *Say No to Guilt! The 21 Day Plan for Accepting Your Chronic Illness and Finding Inner Peace and Happiness*

- *Say Yes to Success Despite Your Chronic Illness: 10 Weeks to Overcoming the Obstacles of Chronic Illness and Finally Achieving What You Want in Life!*

- *Wean That Kid: Your Comprehensive Guide to Understanding and Mastering the Weaning Process*
- *I'm a Weaned Kid Now*

Her upcoming publications include:

- *Emergency Income Streams: How to Create Fast Cash in 14 Days or Less*